The Retailer's Guide to Lease Negotiation and Administration in Australia

Hymie Zawatzky

NOTE:

This is a guide. It is not a substitute for obtaining legal advice about your lease, finances or taxation. Nor is it a replacement for a qualified financial advisor. You are encouraged to seek such legal and financial advice where necessary.

DISCLAIMER

At the time of going to press, all information in this book was accurate as the author was able to ascertain within reason. All references to private or state organisations are gratuitous. The author has no financial interest in them and does nor stand to benefit from them in any way

Veritax Business Consultants Pty Ltd
16 Eildon Street
Doncaster Vic 3108
Australia

WEBSITE: www.placeofbooks.com

Cover Design and typeset by BookPOD

Cover Image: iStockphoto

ISBN: 978-0-9873302-5-3 (pbk)

eISBN: 978-0-9873302-6-0 (ebook)

A Catalogue-in-Publication is available from the National Library of Australia.

Contents

A note from the author

My 25 years of experience assisting retailers with lease negotiations has led me to write this practical guide to assist all retailers to ensure their negotiation of a fair lease.

In addition, I bring to this book my many years of experience of lease administration of retail chains and the management of occupancy costs.

Whether you are an existing retailer, own a retail chain, a new operator from overseas bringing your business to Australia, a professional working in a retail environment or a first time migrant retailer seeking a franchise in Australia, this book will I am sure, be of value to you.

This information will be useful as a handbook for universities and technical colleges teaching retail studies. The understanding that occupancy costs are the largest costs of running a retail business, and ways to control these costs will be invaluable to retail students.

Readers please note that this book a guide, and it is not a substitute for obtaining legal advice about your lease should the circumstances require it. Remember, lease negotiation may not always result in the retailer's requirements being met in full. A compromise between what you want, and what the landlord is prepared to give, is often the best solution.

Good reading!

Introduction

Are you in retail?

Do you believe that you do not have a fair lease for your store?

Is renewing your lease every 5 years giving you as headache?

Are you paying too much rent?

Do you wish that you knew how to negotiate a better lease with your landlord?

Are you thinking of bringing your business to Australia?

Are you considering selling your business?

Do you know how to ensure that the annual outgoings charged by the landlord is fair and reasonable and complies with the provisions of the Retail Tenancy Act in your state?

Are you studying about retail at a college or university?

Do you know the law covering franchisees and franchisors from both a state and federal perspective?

If the answer to any of these questions is "Yes" then this book is for you.

What is this book all about?

This book is an essential handbook to help you to negotiate your lease and administer it during the lease term, whether you are:

- A small retailer in a shopping centre or in strip of shops.

- A chain of retail stores.

- A supermarket or department store.

- A franchisee, where the lease is in the name of the franchisor.

- A professional like a pharmacist or optometrist trading in a retail environment but having to abide by professional regulations,

- An international chain coming to Australia.

In an industry dominated by a dozen or so major shopping centre owners it is essential for the retailer to negotiate professionally. The retailer needs to be fully aware of the protection given to him under the Retail Tenancy Acts in Australia, as well as those clauses permitted in leases and those that are not.

1

What are the 8 golden rules of negotiating a retail lease?

Negotiating a retail lease is not the result of mere luck but comes from sound and active management.

How to negotiate a retail lease

1. Do your homework and know the rentals being paid by other tenants in your area.

2. Scrutinise all aspects of your lease. Ask relevant questions and make certain that you finalise all aspects of your lease during negotiation, so that the final lease reflects the agreement of all parties involved and has no surprises.

3. In resolving lease issues, the best approach is to think like a landlord and not a retailer. This may not be easy to do, but will provide you with an excellent outcome.

4. Always think ahead and consider what the impact of deregulation on your retail store will be.

5. Fitting out costs are expensive so request the landlord to make a fit-out contribution to this cost.

6. Take into account all the hidden costs involved. These include legal fees, stamp duty, consulting fees, design fees, plan approval fees,

survey fees, lease registration, lease preparation fees as well as any sundry costs.

7. If you are taking over a lease on the purchase of a retail store, always ask a consultant to make a proper due diligence check of the lease to ensure that you have at least five years of the lease outstanding.

8. If you have an interest in a number of retail stores, ensure that you have a corporate structure in place, so that if one store fails your other stores are not affected as well.

2

What is a retail lease?

A retail lease is a document for a pre-negotiated period of time allowing a retailer, in exchange for the payment of rental, to occupy premises owned by a landlord. If at the end of the period the landlord decides that he does not wish to renew the lease there is nothing to stop him letting the premises to someone else. This is an important point to remember as many people enter into lease agreements with the expectation that they will be offered a lease renewal.

Parties to a lease

There are a number of participants involved in any lease negotiation for a retail tenancy. It is important to realize that what each participant seeks to gain from the negotiations is different and will quite often be in conflict.

The participants to any retail lease negotiations are namely:-

A. The Landlord/Lessor

Generally the landlord seeks to secure the following from the lease negotiations:

- An optimum rental for the available space with minimum expenditure. He expects the retailer to be responsible for paying as much of the maintenance and the costs of upkeep as possible.

- The landlord seeks a retailer who has the resources to pay the rent and outgoings over the term of the lease.

- The landlord will seek a watertight lease ensuring that his rights are fully protected. As the landlord is responsible for preparing the lease it is often initially written by the landlord in favour of the landlord.

Landlords generally fall into 3 categories:

- Landlords of retail shopping centres, complexes or malls.

- Landlords of single shops, who are often private investors with properties in strips or stand-alone premises.

- Landlords who own commercial properties that may have shops located in a specific area, such as shops on the ground floor of buildings.

If the premises are in Victoria this may include landlords who have tenants on the first three levels of a commercial building who sell goods and services and who may be covered by the Retail Tenancy Legislation in Victoria. Some of the tenants maybe accounting or legal firms

The Australian Capital Territory is the only state in which there is a commercial business zoning under retail tenancy legislation. The zoning covers retail premises with an area of less than $300m^2$ that are not involved in the sale or hire of goods to fall under the retail tenancy legislation. This zoning usually does not apply to shopping centres.

B. The Retailer/Lessee

Lease negotiations usually allows a retailer or business proprietor to assess whether the conditions will permit the profitable operation of a business, and the development of the goodwill value of that business. As a result, the retailer will be seeking the following key aspects from the lease:

- The ability to conduct a profitable business.

- An affordable rent for the duration of the lease.

- Security of tenure for the desired time.

- Protection from competition, particularly if the retail premises are in a shopping centre or even a strip centre where a number of shops are owned by the same landlord.

- Conditions in the lease that will ensure non-interference in the day to day running of the business.

- Conditions that will not impose additional financial burdens on the business.

- The ability to sell the business and assign the lease with as few problems as possible so as to maximize the goodwill built up in the business.

The letting agent is often the first port of call for many retailers seeking retail premises in a non-shopping centre environment. However, a number of the larger real estate agents also manage and lease space in small shopping centres. The agent often handles all the initial documentation during the negotiation process and usually receives a fee from the landlord for entering into the lease. The agent usually has an administration agreement with the landlord and carries out various duties as agreed upon with the landlord.

Some of the recent changes to retail tenancy legislation, particularly in Victoria, now impose on the agent, the same responsibilities and liabilities as the landlord

D. The Solicitor

There are usually two solicitors that act for parties to a lease. One is employed by the landlord and he will prepare the lease from the commercial lease offer negotiated by the landlords leasing executive or the landlord's agent. The other, is the solicitor for the retailer who advises on the retailer's legal position. Many retailers engage the services of a leasing consultant to help negotiate the lease and prepare a commercial report on the lease document written by the landlord's solicitor. Frequently the consultant's report is combined with the one presented by the retailer's solicitor.

In the case of franchisees, the retailer's solicitor will often prepare the franchise agreement at the same time, so that its duration may coincide with the term of the lease.

E. Assignors and Assignees

If a retailer wishes to sell the business during the term of the lease he or she will become known as the assignor. This means that he or she and will require the approval from the landlord for the assignment of the remainder of the lease to the purchaser of the business.

The law relating to retail tenancies in Australia

The Australian Constitution provides that the states and territories have the power to enact retail tenancy legislation. In Australia the laws relating to retail tenancies can differ between jurisdictions.

It is important for retailers to be aware that if they were to open a retail store in another state, they may find that a number of clauses dealing with rent, outgoings, market reviews, tenancy mix and a number of other clauses may vary from state to state, even when the landlord may be the same.

Types of leases entered into by retailers

A retailer in a shopping centre needs to appreciate that a shopping centre has a broad tenancy mix and that landlords enter into different leases. This depends on the type of tenant you are - a specialty store, a pharmacy, a coffee shop, a supermarket or a mini major department store.

Some of these leases will have the protection of the Retail Tenancy legislation and others will not. The key to this protection by the Act is that if a clause in the lease is contrary to the provisions of the Act, then the wording of that clause is void. Therefore if there is a dispute the provisions of the Act will apply.

There are a number of basic lease conditions that the parties to a lease cannot negotiate or contract out of. These include the minimum lease term, charging of legal expenses, conditions dealing with relocation or demolition of the premises, methods of calculating market rents, methods of calculating outgoings and restrictions on assignment .The Acts specifically cover all these provisions.

In the case of a departmental store or supermarket, the leases will usually be based on a nominal base rent per month or/plus a percentage on sales, whichever is the higher. These leases usually provide for rates and taxes to be paid additionally together with certain specified outgoings attributable to that tenancy. Particularly, large outgoing costs like management fees, centre management costs and security costs are often specifically excluded.

For stores of a size of around 400 square meters plus, (known as mini majors) the lease will usually be based on a low rent per square metre plus a full share of outgoings or even a gross rent comprising the two.

For specialty stores, the lease will usually be calculated on a much higher rent per sq. metre as well as a full share of outgoings. Jewellery shops and fashion operators tend to pay the highest rental per square meter in a shopping centre as do food outlets. However, the food outlets generally occupy only a small area.

Stores in strip centres usually have only a base rent component plus statutory municipal charges and land tax. Sometimes insurance is also payable. Land tax is specifically legislated not to be paid in some states by retailers under the Act.

Figures from URBIS, (which are often quoted by landlords in negotiations as the benchmark for your retail category) shows that sometimes, group retail categories are linked together such as pharmacies with cosmetics. Any pharmacist will know that these are two completely different market sectors. It is well documented that cosmetic stores have smaller retail footprints and even have "island locations" in the middle of the mall. These formats have higher rentals. Thus, combining this format with pharmacy data increases the average rental per square metre giving misleading information regarding "expected rents". Other retailers in similar situations need to watch out for similar groupings.

What name is the lease to be entered into?

It is important to carefully consider the entity that will enter into the lease on behalf of the retailer, for example a private company, public company, trust, partnership or a store in the name of an individual or partnership.

In the case of a private company the directors of the private company may have to guarantee the lease. In the event of an individual or partnership, each individual automatically guarantees the lease with all his or her private assets. These assets would become available to be taken by the lessor in the event of a default of the lease.

If you are for example, a pharmacist, naturopath, psychologist or optometrist forming part of a medical clinic, (that is in a shopping centre or in a stand-alone clinic) you may only be a sub-lessee of one of the doctors who holds the head lease. It is therefore imperative that your sub-lease is structured in a way that it allows you or the other medical professionals to go in and out of the clinic, without disturbing the lease. It may be prudent to secure the lease in the name of a management company or service company for the clinic with each participant holding a share in the management or service-company.

The most asked question by retailers before in entering into the lease is "how much is the rent? The answer is not that simple, as landlords may require a number of components that make up the final total rent payable. So, read the small print of your lease and disclosure statement very carefully.

3

Retail rent

What is rent?

The courts have defined rent as follows: "A sum of money that a person has contracted to pay for the use of property for a term". The way a retailer structures the payment of rent can often determine how profitable the business may be.

The best type of rent package that can be negotiated by a retailer is a gross rent deal. (This would include a total occupancy figure covering rent, statutory and variable outgoings.) If rent is payable in a shopping centre it would include the marketing levy as well. It is important for the retailer to know exactly what the total rental will be without any additional charges.

The next best rent package to be considered, is one in which the retailer pays a negotiated net rent amount and where the outgoings for the current year are considered to be the "base_amount_". Outgoings during the lease period are only payable on the proportion of the amount in excess of the base amount when the lease was entered into.

Most speciality leases are based on an agreed cost per sq. metre plus outgoings based on the proportion that the area of the retailers shop bears to the gross lettable area of the centre or complex.

Rent free periods

As an inducement to a retailer to enter into a lease, a landlord may offer the retailer a rent free period in the first year. This will allow the retailer an initial cash saving to be set off against the high cost of fitting out and stocking the store.

Such incentives have become quite common particularly when existing shopping centres are being refurbished and the landlord is trying to attract new types of tenants to the centre.

Rent free periods are also frequently offered where a store has remained unoccupied for some time and the landlord is keen to attract a good retailer.

Therefore, a retailer should always try to negotiate an initial rent free period of about 3 to 6 months. This will allow trading properly before rent is payable. The downside is that the retailer will have to contribute to outgoings from day one.

Percentage rent payable

Some shopping centre leases usually include an additional rental known as percentage rental. This rental is usually calculated on an agreed percentage of sales (depending on the industry) less the base rental. It is often regarded by a retailer as an attempt by the landlord to gain additional rental if the business is successful and achieves better than projected sales.

As these percentage rents are structured around a base rental, this effectively means that the landlord is sharing the good times of a retail store without sharing any of the risks. It has become standard management practice in leases to have percentage rent clauses.

This is an example of how the percentage rental is calculated	
Sales for Year are	$500,000
Agreed percentage rental	8%
Base rent for Year	$38,000
Thus percentage rent is calculated as follows	
$500000 x 8%	$40,000
Less Base Rental for year	$38,000
Percentage Rent Payable	$2000

From a landlord's perspective, receiving some annual percentage rental may be valuable, however this is not the entire reason for this clause. Landlords under the various Retail Tenancy Acts in Australia are not permitted to ask the tenants to provide the sales of the business. By using this technique of a percentage rental clause they are thus entitled to obtain the retailer's sales figures annually. In this way they can check if any percentage rental is payable.

Calculating the percentage rent allows the landlord or the agent to determine what rental the tenant can afford in future lease negotiations and at the same time allow the landlord to do planning for the future management and development of the centre.

Pharmacy retailers could argue that they cannot pay percentage rent as the Pharmacy Act prevents a retailer from sharing his or her income with someone who is not a retailer as provided in Section 92© Pharmacy Practice Act 2004 (Victoria).

The pharmacy retailer may on the other hand agree to provide sales figures based on the front of shop sales plus NHS revenue (not the value of the scripts). Many shopping centre landlords are operating on this principle.

Annual rent reviews

Most leases provide for a regular annual review of rents with no ceiling on the amount of the increase or decrease. These so called "ratchet clauses" (where rents could only go up) have now been abolished in all states.

Under the retail legislation it is a requirement that a clearly defined formula be set out in the lease document for example 5% fixed increase per annum or CPI or a market review. In some states CPI + 2.%. This combination is not permitted in Victoria.

If the formula is not included specifically in the lease then no variation of rent is possible unless all parties agree.

Given that CPI increases are not common for all states, a retailer in Perth for example, may have a larger CPI base than a retailer in Melbourne. To smooth out fluctuations for a retailer operating in a number of states it may be useful for him to request that the CPI formula to be used will be the average CPI over the eight capital cities and not the CPI of the city where the store is located.

Am I being asked to pay a reasonable rent?

This is a particularly important question to ask if the terms of the lease includes a market review of rent in years four of a five of the lease.

Before agreeing to the final rent and outgoings that a retailer believes he or she can afford to pay the retailer should prepare a profit and loss statement over the full period of the lease, showing anticipated sales growths and gross profit projections.

To do this you deduct your anticipated labour costs, advertising and other store expenses as well as the anticipated store profit you are budgeting for. This will show a balance that represents the profit you can anticipate you can earn before occupancy costs. Then add in the occupancy cost showing the impact of possible high, medium and low market rent review scenarios.

If a retailer cannot achieve the anticipated profit percentage to sales that he is budgeting for using the high market review scenario during the lease term, the initial base year rent and outgoings' negotiation with the landlord will have to be reviewed. This is a sure sign that the landlord is asking for a premium for being in that centre that is over and above what you can probably afford.

Option renewals and exercising your option under the terms of the lease

Your management schedule (see chapter 19 in this book on how this is prepared) will alert you to the date by which you need to exercise your option.

Remember that an option in a lease is a right that every retailer has and it is not the right of the landlord. The retailer alone can decide whether he will exercise the option or not.

The landlord may be anxious until the retailer formally exercises the option. He will be uncertain whether the retailer will continue in occupation or whether he will have to find a new retailer, even at a reduced rental. Retailers often may use this opportunity to improve conditions in their lease by requesting the landlord to vary certain lease conditions. Certain problem clauses may be altered at this stage, due to the landlord's vulnerability.

However, the retailer's ability to take advantage of the situation is likely to be determined by the way the parties negotiated the original option terms of the leas.

Retailers should not accept a clause that grants an option in the lease but which further provides for the cancellation of this option should the landlord wish to redevelop or refurbish that part of the shopping centre.

Retailers should avoid types of clauses that provide for "due and punctual performance" of all of the terms and conditions of the lease throughout the term as a pre-condition to the exercise of an option. The retailer's solicitor should water down such a clause to ensure that the retailer can exercise such option, if he or she is not in breach of the lease (at the time of the notice exercising the option or at the expiration of the term of the lease).

4

Outgoings

Negotiating outgoings payable by the retailer

Most leases are based on a base rental plus outgoings, therefore, it is essential that all retailers understand exactly what this entails.

In a shopping centre all the retail Acts require the landlord to provide the retailer with a schedule of outgoings that forms part of the pool of outgoings. Based on this schedule, the tenant will be required to pay outgoings to the landlord. The payment is usually monthly, based on a rate per square metre for such outgoings.

As the rate for outgoings in some larger shopping centres is now more than $225 per square metre, this is an extremely important component of the total rental package.

Advice for retailers:

When the landlord quotes you an outgoings rate per square metre, you should ensure that you know precisely which outgoings that rate covers.

Some outgoings schedules include municipal council and water rates and if applicable a land tax charge, while others do not. If these outgoings are excluded from the rate, you will probably be billed either directly by the state authority or the centre will pay the account and recover it from the retailer periodically throughout the financial year.

When calculating your occupancy cost before signing the lease make sure that you include all outgoing charges both "direct and indirect ".

Remember that in some states like Queensland, South Australia and Victoria, land tax is no longer recoverable as an outgoing from retailers. Therefore, make certain that you are given a current schedule of outgoings with your disclosure statement and ask your solicitor to check that each item on the schedule is covered by a corresponding clause in the lease. This ensures that in later years any new outgoing expense cannot be included without your permission.

The management and administration charge of the centre is one of the largest outgoings expenses charged by the landlord. Ask the landlord to tell you exactly how this cost is made up. He should tell you the precise amount represented by centre management, salaries, wages and office expenses In addition, he should reveal how the "basis" of the corporate head office was calculated , as well as the "basis" that the corporate head office expenses was allocated between all the shopping centre owned by that landlord.

Note that in West Australia management fees are not recoverable as an outgoing from retailers and in Victoria management fees are capped by the increase in CPI for the year.

Air conditioning

Air Conditioning costs and their apportionment to retailers has become a source of contention between the landlord and the retailer.

Although one centralised system seems to service the entire centre, landlords contend that the major anchor tenants have their own air-conditioning systems and as a result their leases do not provide for them having to bear any share of the air-conditioning expenses. Naturally, this has resulted in an imbalance in the area proportion over which such costs are made.

Repairs and maintenance

Repairs and Maintenance is another large expense in the outgoing schedule. It is advisable to obtain a breakdown of how these costs are calculated into building repairs, electrical, signs, car parks, locks and keys, glass and so on.

In Victoria the Act has been changed to make landlords more responsible for paying for repairs and maintenance. These costs should not be included in the outgoings schedule payable by the tenant. In addition any costs in respect of the safety of the building has also been deemed to be the expense of the landlord and not an outgoing (however this is still under appeal in the courts).

Alert yourself to the possibility of capital expenditure being included in this outgoing cost particularly where a shopping centre is under refurbishment.

If you are in a strip centre that may be subject to flooding from storms, always insist that the lease contains a condition requiring the landlord to ensure that the premises are water and weather sealed on the handover of the premises.

Typical retailers checklist of outgoings each year

A. Gross lettable area

* Is the G.L.A the same as it was in the previous year?

* If not, establish the reasons for change.

* Check the G.L.A reconciliation form to establish whether the landlord has changed the basis of calculating the G.L.A.

* Does the G.L.A. as calculated, conform to the definition in the lease and disclosure statement? This is a key point.

- If renovations or refurbishments are taking place in the centre over the 30th June period, check whether any additional area has been taken into account in determining the GLA calculation in the budget provided by the centre.

- If there are free-standing tenancies at the centre, for example service stations, fast food outlets and so on, check if these have been taken into account in the GLA calculation.

- Has the office area of the shopping centre been deducted from the GLA? Some landlords have taken legal opinion that has not as yet been challenged. Challenge this if you are in doubt.

- Have the number of kiosks in the centre remained the same as last year? If kiosks are removed then this area should be included in the common area and deducted from GLA. If new kiosks are erected GLA should increase and the common area should be decreased.

B. Retailers own demised premises

- Has the size of your premises changed from last year?

- Is the size of your premises still as stated in the lease? If not you should have confirmation on file to this effect. This may include downsizing of premises during the year.

- If the size of your premises is calculated on a percentage of the total centre, always check the reference schedule of your lease to see how many decimal places the calculation is to be computed. This may seem a minor matter but mistakes are often made to the retailer's detriment.

- The outgoings apportionment should be on same basis as stated in the reference schedule in the lease.

-

- Be certain that the same percentage is used in apportionment from year to year. If the centre has not increased in size this should reduce your percentage.

C. Variable outgoings – a general check list

Take the following steps to ascertain any variances in the outgoings you are charged.

- From the schedule supplied to you by the centre management, prepare a comparison between the current year's outgoings and the following budget year and note any variances.

- On receipt of the actual audited outgoings, prepare a comparison between the actual and the budget for the year and note any variances.

- Then prepare a comparison of the actual audited outgoings for the previous year with the budget for the following year and note any variances.

- Compare the above variances with the assumptions made by the centre in the preparation of the budget in order to ensure that the data is still valid. If you detect a major variance that is not in your favour, request an explanation from centre management. If an unsatisfactory explanation is given, request that the budget is revised providing you with a saving in cash flow during the budget year.

- Check the outgoings that you have been charged with the actual lease provisions. If the charge is not specifically contained in the lease, raise a query with the centre. If the charge is due to interpretation of the lease wording, query this as well. In Victoria the outgoings must benefit the premises in order to be able to be charged to the retailer. Therefore, if your premises are on the outside of a centre you should not have to pay for escalators or air conditioning.

- If you have more than one retail store, compare your analysis of the above points with the landlord's other centres to see if any common trend emerge. This will alert you to the possibility of errors in the charges.

- If there were any concessions obtained or negotiated with the landlord in a previous year, ascertain that they have carried forward to the budget year.

- If your retail store trades outside the normal working hours of the centre for example, until 9pm each night, you should try to negotiate that your specific trading hours stated in the lease is separate from the centre's basic trading hours, so that any costs after the centre's normal trading hours are not charged to you. This is often applicable to video shops and pharmacists who often trade after normal trading hours.

- If you are trading outside normal trading hours of the centre and are forced to pay a fee per hour to the centre for this, you need to ensure that you are not paying twice. Check whether this payment for after-hours expenses was deducted from the pool of outgoings before the balance of the pool is allocated to tenants.

D. Variable outgoings - specific expenses in shopping centres

Tenants in strip centres or in stand- alone locations, often only pay rates and taxes and insurance costs. Tenants in shopping centres are usually charged the following costs. The Tenancy Acts in most states usually state the amount that can be charged and any unusual costs or the charge for "sundry costs" should immediately be questioned.

1. Security

- Some landlords include a proviso, after the preamble to the outgoings clause that management's responsibility includes " operation and management," of the centre. This includes security of the centre.

- As you are paying for security you should insist that your lease or leases include the words" and securing the centre". This may assist your insurance company in recovering a theft claim if the centre fails to provide adequate security.

2. Air Conditioning

- Ensure that the cost of air conditioning of cinemas will be borne directly by the cinema operator. Also ensure that the cost of air-conditioning of cinema foyers are not included with common areas of the centre.

- Be aware that electricity charges for running air conditioning plants can be purchased by the centre at bulk rates and charged to retailers at normal rates. A good way of finding out if this is happening would be to compare your store electricity costs per square metre with the common area cost to see if there is a difference.

3. Cleaning

- Note that the expense of cleaning may include salary costs of the cleaner employed by the centre. Unless the lease provides otherwise, ensure that only the basic salary is charged and there are no provisions made for long service or annual leave.

- Cleaning may include waste removal. If your lease specifically excludes "wet refuse", ensure that this is deducted.

- Check to see if cleaning costs include cleaning of food courts and salary costs of waitressing for common areas. Most new leases should provide for such costs to be borne by food court retailers directly.

- Often food court expenses are charged to food court operators as a "marketing levy" based on the total cost divided by the number of food court operators. This avoids the provisions of the Tenancy Acts that requires the costs to be charged to retailers on the basis that the ratio of the area of the store bears to the area of the centre.

- If the centre includes an office tower, check the apportionment of cost between common areas of each floor of offices and centre common areas.

- Note that In New South Wales cleaning has to be split by the landlord between cleaning costs and consumable cleaning expenses.

4. Insurance

- Establish the basis of insurance apportionment for groups of landlords who have a portfolio of properties. Often this basis is established on the value of buildings. If a landlord has a major property and the value has fallen dramatically in other centres including a centre where your store is located, he may be absorbing a higher insurance allocation.

- In the case of centres owned by insurance companies, establish how the insurance cost was determined and whether the cost is an internal charge or it represents a true market charge.

- If insurance rates have generally fallen in Australia, enquire why a particular centre has not followed the national trend. Your own insurer is often a good source of information.

- The high cost of public liability insurance needs to be carefully examined by lease administrators. For instance, major landlords who operate on a worldwide basis have in the past been hard hit by terrorism threats in the USA and Europe. As a result their world insurance costs were increased. This is also the case in Australian centres though Australia may not have the same risks as Europe or the USA.

- Any excess on a claim that is to be borne by the lessor can sometimes be included in the insurance estimate given to the tenant. Check to see whether this is the case at your centre.

5. Car Parking

- Car Parking costs should normally only include line marking and other minor costs. If the amount is greater than $5000 query this cost. You should not have to pay for the costs of asphalting the car park every few years as this is a capital cost.

- If the car park is let to a private contractor, an area of the car park should be classified as GLA and not as common area. The cost of running the car park becomes that of the private contractor and not the tenants of the centre.

6. Energy Costs

- Some major tenancies use substantial quantities of electricity after normal hours trading (for example cinemas, railway stations etc) and are often charged separately for this by the lessor. Check that any reimbursement by these operators is deducted from your total energy costs before it has been apportionment to you.

- Test check the tariff ratings you have been charged. You need to ensure that you are paying the best tariff rate at all times, particularly as shopping centres operate extensively outside normal office hours

7. Lifts and Escalators

- The energy costs to run the lifts and escalators are usually determined on an "allocated basis" by the lessor from the total electricity costs. The same principles apply as those on the air conditioning checklist.

- Some old leases refer to payments for lifts only. If a centre has been redeveloped and now includes escalators and travelators, you must determine whether you will accept the costs for this extended range of equipment.

- If a bank of lifts services an office tower, alongside it or part of the centre complex, query whether you should pay for these costs particularly if the offices are excluded from GLA.

8. Repairs and Maintenance

- If the centre has recently been refurbished, check for sudden increases in budgeted repairs and maintenance. Some landlords may try to apply post construction problems to repairs and maintenance outgoings.

- Investigate jumps in this cost in the year after a refurbishment since these costs they may now include maintenance agreements on equipment previously under guarantee

- Salary costs of maintenance staff are usually included in this item. Ascertain from store management if maintenance staff have been fully occupied in that centre. If not ask how the cost was apportioned.

9. Gardening and Landscaping

- If the gardening and landscaping outgoing includes indoor plants, ensure that the capital cost of the pots is not added to the maintenance charge.

- Periodically check with store management whether the centre does actually have gardens. This will assist in testing whether the charge is reasonable.

- Some leases provide for gardening to include "areas in the vicinity of the centre". The landlord could claim that this land is future redevelopment land that it has to be maintained according to the council's directive. However, in many cases the cost is simply passed onto the tenant. Remember, this land is not part of the common area of the centre on which outgoings are payable.

- Ensure that any landscaping costs are not of a capital nature. The test to employ is that the cost must not enhance the value of the centre but instead maintain the appearance of the centre.

10. Management Expenses

See more in the following detailed analysis.

11. Miscellaneous Expenses

- If the expense is over $5000, ascertain whether this cost includes a "community charge". This outgoings charge is usually attributable to say a library in the centre that does not pay outgoings as per its lease, and whose outgoings are then included in the other retailers outgoings pool.

- If this cost is excessive check whether it includes any capital costs such as a new motor car for the centre manager.

- Some landlords purchase items as part of an operating lease or hire agreements. They then turn these costs that are not recoverable as an outgoing, into recoverable expenses by using this technique. Watch out for this.

- Note that in Victoria Section 41 of the Act specifically defines capital expenditure as non-recoverable from retailers "on any areas used in association with a building and plant in a building"

12. Hydraulics/ Equipment Hire

This expense cost classification is used in the main by one major property group.

- Equipment hire usually includes scissor lifts and cherry picker equipment hired for roofs and lighting repairs, and are genuine outgoings.

- Be aware that this expense has now also become a dumping ground for lease back deals of shopping centre assets.

13. Outside the Lease Terms - "Acceptable" Outgoings

- From time to time a retailer may negotiate as a "trade off" for other considerations by the landlord to pay for outgoings outside the provisions of the lease.

- Ensure that all these acceptable outgoings are authorised, fully documented and   maintained with lease records.

Occasionally, check to see if the circumstances that gave rise to this additional outgoings cost, have changed.

Management fees

Victoria - background

Section 49 of the Retail Leases Act 2003 places a limit on the recovery of management fees from retailers who are subject to the Act

1. Section 49 provides that such increase must not exceed CPI.

2. The landlord's budgeted outgoings charged for the year must be sent to the retailer by 31 May each year. The only CPI index available is the CPI calculation for the March quarter, which is the percentage that must be used rather than an estimate by the landlord.

3. Some landlords for whom this has been queried respond by stating that it is merely a budget and the true management fees which are often a percentage of centre rentals will only be known at the end of the year. As the section is clearly applicable when "the retailer is liable to pay" it seems logical that the "cap" applies when the retailer starts to make payments in terms of the budgeted outgoings.

4. When the actual management fees are determined for the year ended 30 June as certified by the auditors, the CPI adjustment will be recalculated to take into account the CPI for the year ended 30 June.

5. Landlords who undertake a substantial redevelopment of a shopping centre (which may entail a major increase in management fees in future years) may be disadvantaged as the Act is silent on this and the base management fee charge subject to CPI once established may not be altered till a new lease is entered into.

Thus during a major redevelopment the landlord will endeavour to put as many existing tenants onto a new lease as possible.

6.   According to Section 49(a) (ii) the management fees must exclude salaries and other administrative costs relating to the operation of that building or shopping centre. These costs are often shown by landlords on the outgoings statements as direct administration costs of the centre, for example centre management salaries, wages and expenses. In addition, there are further fees namely management fees.

7.   This raises the question of what remains in "management fees" after deducting salaries and wages and so on. Are management fees merely an arbitrary outgoing charge by the landlord to increase their revenue without it being an actual reimbursement of a cost actually incurred? Outgoings are meant to be costs that have been incurred.

8.   Retailers with a retail lease where the premises are located in a shopping centre are only liable to contribute to the outgoing of the landlord under the following circumstances:

•   If it benefits specific retail premises in the centre and that retail tenancy benefits the retailers premises

•   If capital costs are not recoverable.

9.   Management fees may include elements of payment for:

•   Development costs of the centre.

•   Leasing fees for the first year's income for new speciality retailers.

•   Fees for marketing and management of major retailers.

- A fee based on a percentage of the assets in the trust, where the centre is owned by a retail trust in Australia (REITS).

- A performance fee if the trust exceeds the growth of the property index on the Australian stock exchange.

Clearly each of these items fall outside the definition of management fees, that can be recovered under the Act as an outgoings from retailers with retail leases in Victoria.

10. Clearly the 10% prescribed amount as set out in regulation 12 of the rules of the Act would possibly require both the landlord and the auditor to show a more detailed breakdown of how these two costs are made up.

West Australia

No management fees may be recovered from a tenant in West Australia. Only the cost of managing the centre, such as centre management expenses, salaries and the cost of a maintenance team may be recovered. More and more leases in shopping centres are being negotiated on a gross deal basis plus statutory charges, thereby incorporating the management fee into the rent.

The repeal of carbon tax and its impact on retailers and landlords (with effect from 1 July 2014)

According to the new legislation carbon tax was repealed with effect from 1 July 2014 and made retrospective to that date.

Impact on outgoings and store costs

1. It is anticipated by the government that electricity costs and retail gas prices that are both high outgoings costs in most outgoings budgets will fall by 9% and 7% respectively in 2014/5.

2.   Since most landlords have issued outgoings budgets either for the year ended 30 June 2015 or for the year ended 31 December 2014, retailers need to inquire whether budgets include carbon tax on electricity and gas or if these charges have been removed. If not you need to request an amended budget to reflect the new legislation.

3.   The government is committed to ensure that consumers benefit from the removal of the carbon tax. The ACCC has been given powers to ensure that in the year following the removal of the tax, they will be able to take action against businesses that engage in carbon tax-related exploitation.

4.   The Office of Treasury estimates that the repeal of the carbon tax could have a 0.7% fall in CPI in the year following the repeal. This will have an effect on retailers who have gross leases that include both base rent and outgoings. Retailers may argue that their rent should be reduced as a result of a major outgoings costs being substantially reduced. However, landlords may argue that as they bore the cost when carbon tax was introduced and no reduction should be made. In West Australia landlords have been prohibited from collecting management fees. Instead many have been charging gross leases plus statutory charges. As they bore the extra costs when the carbon tax was introduced, they may be reluctant to renegotiate leases.

5.   One of the largest outgoing costs in many centres is council rates. When carbon tax was initially introduced, councils estimated that charges for carbon tax would be around 4% particularly for councils with high waste management costs as well as the cost of large landfill sites. At present a number of councils are uncertain about ways in which to reduce the rates to cover liabilities. Many have simply reduced the rate charge by 4%. Retailer and landlords may have to pressurize councils to drop the charge of council rates and waste management or appeal to the ACCC to investigate this.

6. Other charges by State Governments need to be investigated by retailers in order to bring down charges. For example, Melbourne Water which is owned by the Victorian Government has already set water prices to include the tax. But this is not due to be reviewed until 2017/18.

7. In Victoria section 49 of the Act also limits the recovery of management fees in the outgoings schedule to CPI. If as stated above and we have a fall in CPI of about .7%, retailers need to ensure that this is the case when they receive their audited outgoings for the 2014/15 year. If there is any discrepancy it should be raised with the landlord's auditors.

8. In leases where the landlord is permitted to purchase electricity at bulk rates and he is charging it out to tenants at single consumer rates, retailers must ensure that the carbon tax element is reduced in both the purchase and on-charge rate.

9. In states where sinking funds are charged as a percentage of outgoings for future maintenance, these will need to be revised as previous outgoing provisions include carbon tax. This could result in a credit to the outgoings budget and a saving for tenants.

5

Fit-out of a retail store

If your shop is in a new centre or the redeveloped area of an existing centre, be certain that you sign a fit-out agreement with your fit-out contractor. The fit-out agreement must clearly spell out the contractor's rights and obligations to ensure these are not in conflict with those of the main builders.

All parties must be clear about the date of hand over of the store to your shopfitter, the date of practical completion, and the date of lease commencement. The dates can be confusing so be careful.

You could be caught up in a situation where the lease commencement date is specified to be the date of practical completion of the centre or the date of the handover of the store for fitting out. In practical terms your fit-out might take another 4 weeks which means your first rent review may be much sooner than you anticipated. (That is after 11 months trading and not 1 year later).

If you have negotiated an incentive deal with the landlord who may have contributed to your fit-out, make sure you are aware of the fittings that will remain the property of the landlord and those that you will be entitled to remove. The taxation implications of this type of incentive are very complicated and you should discuss it with your tax adviser.

Clauses to be included in contracts and orders awarded to fit-out contractors

In accepting the order from the retailer, the fit-out contractor should acknowledge and confirm the following conditions appertaining to the contract awarded:

- We understand and have received confirmation from the retailer as to the date the fit-out is to be completed. We further acknowledge that time is of the essence in the completion of the contract and that the contractor has sufficient resources and manpower to complete the fit-out on time.

- The price contained in the agreement is a fixed price and any variations will only be payable with the prior agreement of the retailer before undertaking such additional works.

- I have read the tenancy design and fit-out guide and do not believe that there are any provisions or conditions in the guide that I cannot meet. In any event I will comply except where there is a conflict.

- I agree to use only new material or as agreed with the retailer.

- I have examined the drawings and specifications and confirm that the proposed fit-out will meet such specifications and designs and will not require any further modification or variation.

- That I have sufficient contractor's insurance to meet the requirements of the agreement to lease and not less than $20 million in public liability.

- I have read and understood the site conditions that apply to the site during my fit-out and I agree to comply with these provisions. Any claims arising out of a breach of such conditions will be for the account of the fit-out contractor without any recourse to the retailer.

- The works will be carried out during normal working hours unless the landlord in his discretion allows access at other times.

- In the event of any disputes I undertake to abide by an architect appointed by the Institute of Architects.

- I am satisfied that the lessor has completed its entire works as contracted for in their agreement to lease prior to fit -out.

- I have obtained all the necessary permits consents and approvals required under law before the retailers works are started or carried out.

- I am satisfied as to the charges to be made to the retailer regarding category one works and will undertake to either agree to such costs or proceed with and assist the retailer to arbitration by a quantity surveyor in term of the Retail Leases Act.

- I agree to keep the premises tidy and clean and on completion of the works to remove all waste and debris wrappings and residual materials which result from the retailer's works.

- I will rectify all damage to the premises or the land or any part of it which are the direct or indirect result of carrying out the retailer's works.

- I agree to indemnify the retailer from any claims arising out of delays caused by, or incidental to the execution of the retailer's works.

- Any designs and intellectual rights regarding the fit-out will remain the property of the retailer at all times.

The document must be signed and dated.

Administering turn-key projects

More and more larger retailers are using a method known as "turn-key" projects to finance the enormous cost of fitting out their stores. In this situation the landlord agrees to fit-out the premises up to a certain amount in exchange for an additional rental.

This means that the retailer receives a minimum interest loan and pays it back monthly by way of rental.

The amount paid back is the same each year and is not subject to rental increases.

The assets up to the amount of the turn- key costs are retained by the lessor as an asset on which they can claim depreciation over the period of the lease.

Before embarking on such a course of action, all parties should discuss this. The tax implications are quite beneficial to each party. (The Jupiter case dealing with interest in such a transaction should be considered in this regard). You must also discuss this course of action with a tax adviser.

The retailer can claim the extra rent as a tax deduction and the landlord gives the retailer what they want. He can claim back the loan by way of a tax deduction as depreciation or a lease incentive in some cases.

This additional rent does not form part of any formula in the lease for purposes of calculating rent. The only way to control leases with this type of financing is to ensure that the lease schedule is structured to show the normal rent as base rent and the turn key rent as special rent. This will allow you to monitor increases and percentage rent calculations accordingly.

Note that GST will be payable on both rentals

Taxation legislation is constantly changing and both parties should keep up to date with any taxation changes.

Taking over the store from the landlord ready for fitting out

Conditions for hand over of premises

The retailer needs to include a clause in the disclosure statement or request confirmation by the lessor that stipulates that he will only agree to take possession of the premises from the lessor as being complete and ready for fit-out, providing the following:

a.   All lessor's works have been completed.

b.   The premises are handed over with a smooth floor in a broom swept condition and with plasterboard ceilings and walls.

c.   There is a supply of water and waste to an electrical point with a basin and tap in accordance with the design criteria.

d.   The sprinkler system including the sprinkler heads are fully installed in line with the design criteria.

e.   There is an electrical board with standard power in line with design criteria.

f.   The air conditioning system and air conditioning registers have been installed to fit in with the design criteria and that the quality of air conditioning provides comfort even when the lighting exceeds 75 watts per square metre of floor area.

g.   The premises are water sealed and weatherproof,

The analysis of responsibility as per leases for fire and emergency equipment

*   Landlords, particularly those of large shopping centres, are currently under extreme pressure from state governments and state

emergency services to ensure that the emergency services and fire equipment within their centres complies with set standards.

- As a result of spiralling insurance costs, landlords have been pressured by risk management departments to ensure that emergency services are properly audited and maintained.

- In states like New South Wales the Council regulations require the shopping centres to provide the councils with a satisfactory Maintenance Essential Services Certificate on a six monthly basis. This certificate must relate to the centre as a whole and must encompass all tenancies.

- In Victoria under regulation standard AS: 2293 a compliance audit of the emergency and exit lighting needs to be conducted every 6 months. This testing must be documented to check that the lighting illuminates the area and that the battery backup operates correctly and successfully powers the emergency and exit lighting for 90 minutes. A logbook to this effect must be kept on the premises.

- A number of major landlords have instituted these emergency systems compliance audits in the shopping centres that they manage. As a result, retailers have been sent a number of letters requesting that they comply either by doing rectification and compliance themselves or by contracting their agents, who will charge for the service. As landlords have begun formal compliance audits and retailers in their centres have been sent letters requesting they adhere to their responsibility, this raises the issue of responsibility for emergency services as required under the lease.

- Most state emergency requirements clearly provide that the owner of the property has the ultimate responsibility for ensuring that fire-fighting equipment is installed and properly maintained. There are severe penalties if this is not adhered to.

- Most of the shopping centres run a building intelligence program that monitors emergency and exit lighting within the centre. Some major landlords have a specific outgoings charge to cover this.

- AMP centres include a "stand-by equipment" charge included in their outgoings which indicates that they have this equipment in all centres. This includes backup generators that will cut in if there is an electricity failure and will then provide emergency lighting. Other landlords probably have similar emergency equipment but do not show it separately as an outgoings charge.

Review of aspects of leases or parts of leases covering the fit-out of the tenancy

A review of most retailer's leases shows the following anomalies:

- The detailed responsibility to inspect, check and pay for emergency services and equipment is often not clearly described in the leases with one or two exceptions.

- Provisions stating that the landlord is required to install fire sprinklers, build the fire wall and install the necessary fire hydrants in the centre are often included in the "Agreement to Lease" under the heading of "Lessors and Lessees" and retailers need to watch for this.

In some leases dealing with sprinklers that the landlord is expected to install in the premises the provisions are stated as follows:

- "The lessor will provide automatic fire sprinklers in accordance with Australian Standard no AS 2118 to suit a clear and empty shell shop; The lessor will install sprinklers heads within the plasterboard ceilings. Any relocation requirement will be to the lessees cost"

- The "Lessees Works" as set out in the "Agreement to Lease", often contains a provision that the retailer is to supply and maintain fire reels and hoses in the tenancy and provide emergency lighting for exits from the store, Clearly this is the retailer's responsibility and he has an obligation to maintain these to the required standard.

Some leases clearly states that the lessee must provide the following in its tenancy:-

- "Fire protection equipment as required by the Building Çode of Australia. - supply and installation of fire extinguishers as required by the CFA. Category 2 works schedules usually defines this further by providing as follows."

- "Supply and Installation in accordance with AS 2.444 requirement of 1 – 2A.20BE dry powder extinguisher to be placed within 2 meters   adjacent to the switchboard or any other special fire fighting equipment (e.g. fire blankets) which may be required by CFA."

Since sprinklers which form part of the common areas they are clearly the responsibility of the landlord. It is assumed that over the course of the year the landlord performs the following services:

- That he has a six monthly inspection of the fire walls and that these are tagged to this effect.

- That he performs a 3 monthly inspection to check that the pressure is correct in the sprinklers and that they will function in the event of an emergency.

- That he also checks all fire hydrant hoses and reels within the common area of the centre at least every three months to ensure than the equipment has not been vandalised and will function in an emergency.

These expenses related to this service by the landlord are included in the outgoings clause of the lease. Tenants usually accept (without seeing proof) that landlords do make these inspections and tests and that the costs are shown on the outgoings statements provided by the landlord.

A good example to illustrate this outgoings recovery charge is the wording in a recent lease clause. It indicates that the lessor may recover from the lessee its share of: "The cost of maintenance, repair and testing of all fire equipment including sprinkler installations, hydrants, fire extinguishers, smoke detectors and fire-fighting equipment installed by the lessor throughout the centre together with charges rendered by any authority in the supply maintenance servicing and monitoring of fire equipment and of attending to fire alarms".

Some retailers however, negotiate a number of gross leases with landlords where variable outgoings are not payable or where only statutory charges are paid. The retailer will not see such charges on any outgoings statement nor have confirmation that the landlord has performed the tests that have been described above.

Furthermore some leases provide that there is to be at least a 500mm gap between stacked goods or products and the sprinklers. Retailers have in the past received notices from landlords indicating that they are in breach of such a requirement. The retailer could be deemed in breach of their lease if this action affects the lessor's insurance.

Recommended action by the retailer

The audit compliance of fire equipment and emergency lighting by landlords is now a fact of life for both landlords and retailers trading in shopping centres, strip complexes or in a free-standing environment.

Retailers are encouraged to engage the services of FSE or any other qualified provider, to inspect their premises to be certain that all fire hoses and reels and emergency exit lighting is functioning. The FSE or other provider needs to give them a certificate to forward to the landlord confirming that they are meeting their responsibilities under the lease.

Retailers must instruct all retail store staff not to stack products to a height, less than 500 mm from the sprinklers.

Even though most centres are smoke free, retailers may have to give consideration to the installation of smoke detectors in their tenancy.

Note that a special condition is included in your lease (not just in the agreement to lease) that spells out the lessors and lessees requirements when dealing with emergency lighting, fire doors, fire hydrants, sprinklers and fire hoses etc as follows:

That the landlord undertakes and confirms to the retailer that:-

• Within the past 6 months your fire doors have been inspected and

• That the pressure to the sprinklers have been checked within the past three months and

• That all hoses and fire hydrants in the common area have been checked.

6

The lease negotiation process

It is vitally important to understand the lease negotiation process and how to secure the best possible lease. The following background information will help you to put the process of lease negotiation in context.

- The lease process usually begins with an inquiry by the retailer to the leasing department of a shopping centre or the managing agent of an empty store advertising the store to rent.

- Sometimes the lease negotiation occurs as a result of a retailer acquiring a business from an existing owner. In this instance the lease is already in place but there may not be a sufficient lease period left.

- Remember the landlord usually grants a lease of five or six years in duration. The landlord does not have to renew the lease at the end of that term. So, buying a business with only a year to go on the lease does not make good business sense, as you could loose your total investment if the landlord decides not renew the lease.

- If the retailer already has a number of stores and is known in the trade, the initial discussion may result from the landlord's leasing agent contacting the retailer with a view to letting the store and negotiating a lease

- Therefore a retailer should always be cautious, and it is absolutely essential that a retailer entering into a lease asks as many questions as possible during this initial period. The retailer should carefully take note of the landlord's responses as this could assist later if there is a problem or if the landlord has made representations to the retailer which are not true or accurate

The following are a list of the possible questions you should ask about the lease. The questions should be directed to the seller of the business, the landlord or his agent.

Q1. What is the cost of rent per square metre?

The rent quoted may be a gross rent or the base rent for the premises plus outgoing and marketing levy. If the latter, always inquire whether the outgoings include all statutory charges.

Some shopping centre landlords exclude council rates and water from their schedule of outgoings as these may be charged directly to the retailer by the council. They are an extra occupancy cost that must be taken into account by the retailer.

Q2. Does the lease have at least 5 years to run until the end of the current lease term?

If possible, request an option for one or two additional lease terms. Such options should be totally unrestricted in their ability to be exercised.

Remember that an option once granted to a retailer cannot be removed by the landlord. Even if the retailer does not intend to exercise the option this will be to your advantage if you are proposing to sell the business down the track.

Q3. Have the premises been surveyed and is there a survey certificate attached to the lease?

As rent and outgoings are measured on a rate per square metre, it is vital that the area, as shown in the lease, is certified correct by a surveyor. There is more information about this point elsewhere in the book

Q4. Is there a cap on the 'making good provision' in the lease or will the buyer be faced with a costly removal expense for partitions and counters as well as the cost of restoring the premises to its original state?

Always take a photo of the premises at the date of handover as it will be useful when "making good" at the end of the lease term.

Q5. If the lease has an option which results in the rent being required to go to market, ascertain what that rental on a market review is likely to be.

This may require an opinion from a valuer as to the likely market rent on a review. Valuers often use the principal of a "kerb side valuation". Though this is not a full valuation, it is highly regarded and often less costly than a full valuation.

The legislation in New South Wales and Queensland allows for an early market review in the case of the sale of the business. New retailers acquiring a business should make use of these provisions.

Q6. When was the existing lease entered into?

If the lease is one that commenced before the introduction of the current State Acts that have greatly increased the protection of retailers, the retailer may be better off requesting a new lease. This will comply with the new Act, in that state, instead of a variation of the existing lease.

Q7. Does any market review have a "ratchet clause"?

Ensure that any market review clause does not have "ratchet clauses". This type of clause only allows rental to rise and not fall following a review. These clauses are now illegal in all states, but maybe still in old leases with multiple options.

Q8. Have you ensured that clauses dealing with repainting and restoration are not at fixed intervals but as and when necessary, or as mutually agreed?

Some leases require the tenant to repaint the store every three years. The cost of repainting is expensive and the retailer should request an amendment to this clause providing for *"painting of the store during the term of the lease will not be at fixed intervals but as and when necessary as mutually agreed by both parties"*

Q9. Have you made certain that no immediate refurbishment of the store is required on assignment?

This cost should always be taken into account by a potential buyer in assessing the purchase price for the store.

Q10.Does the lease contain a percentage rental clause?

Note that stores in strips and stand-alone stores usually do not have percentage rental clauses.

Q11.If the retail store is situated in a regional shopping centre, does the total gross rent comprising base rent, variable outgoings, statutory charges and marketing contribution exceed your acceptable industry standard?

There are a number of publications that set out these standards along the average gross rental payments by other retailers in similar categories are making.

Also make sure that your type of business is placed in the correct category as different businesses pay different levels of rental in the same shopping centre.

As part of the negotiation process the landlord will normally give the lessee a number of documents namely:

- A disclosure statement.

- A proposed lease offer form.

- A draft copy of the lease.

- An agreement to lease.

- A copy of the lease information document as supplied by the State Government, if applicable.

- A draft plan of the proposed store.

- If the store is in a shopping centre he will provide a list of retailers.

- If you are going into a new shopping centre, you may even receive a marketing brochure of the proposed new shopping centre development.

- A fit-out guide.

Tips during the negotiation process

- Preparation is the key to the lease negotiation process.

- With the knowledge you have gained from this book and the knowledge about the rights given to you under the retail tenancy acts in the state where you are to operate your store,(if you are under the Act) you will be equipped to begin the negotiation process with the landlord or his agent.

- Do not be afraid to quote your rights to the landlord where appropriate.

- Take all emotion out of the negotiation process. Being aggressive if things are not going well is a mistake and shows weakness. Remain detached if possible.

- Think like a landlord and try to see his point of view. This will help you to work out counter arguments.

- Ascertain in advance the true market value of the rent in that shopping centre or strip centre by seeking information from your future retail neighbours. Retailers are usually helpful to new shop owners and will probably tell you what rent they are paying.

- Tricky negotiations may require alternative solutions. Try to put forward a number of alternative proposals, one of which may be mutually acceptable to both parties.

- Do not simply accept responses from the landlord's solicitor as final. Do not be afraid to object and propose alternatives for consideration. Keep the process going, until you arrive at a mutually acceptable conclusion.

- Overseas retailers coming to Australia must take into account that the Australian lease negotiating process may be totally different to what is experienced in their home country. It would be advisable to use a local retail lease consultant who knows the local process, to act on the retailers behalf.

7

Disclosure statements

Current legislation in all states has made the disclosure statement between landlord and retailer the fundamental document in ensuring transparency and proper disclosure of all facts prior to entering into a lease.

Retailers must always insist on being given a lessor's disclosure statement containing all the information as described in the schedule attached to the Acts in all states. Failure to supply a disclosure statement in Victoria allows the retailer to avoid rent payments until one is received.

Remember that the details as contained in the statement continue to be considered factual throughout the term of the lease and throughout the term of any renewal options contained in the original lease. If any of the information given is misleading, the retailer may recover damages.

It cannot be emphasized enough how vital it is that you insist on all details and representations given to you by the landlord or his representative during the negotiation phase, be included in the disclosure statement.

Key points about the new uniform disclosure statement

The states of Victoria, New South Wales and Queensland have agreed on a single uniform landlord disclosure statement. The statement that applies in these states comes into effect on 1 July 2011. Other states have introduced their own disclosure statements that do not differ from this new uniform disclosure statement.

Why the change?

It was anticipated that the nationally integrated form of disclosure statement will have benefits for both tenants and landlords.

Tenants will benefit from the increased disclosure by landlords regarding certain provisions in the retail leases acts. They will be better informed of their rights and obligations under the lease and thereby may make improved decisions about their business. This will also help them to decide whether they still wish to enter into a lease.

Landlords will benefit from a reduced regulatory burden, particularly those landlords who own and operate shopping centres in multiple states.

However as the retail leases Acts remain separate in each state the implications and consequences of the new disclosure statement may still affect tenants differently in each of the three states.

What has changed?

The most fundamental change is the abolition of separate disclosure statements for a shopping centre and a non-shopping centre building or tenancy. In the case of a shopping centre tenancy, additional information is required.

What has not changed?

- The new disclosure statement and lease must still be given to the tenant at least seven days before the lease is entered into.

- If a tenant has not been given a disclosure statement he may give the landlord or his agent no earlier than 7 days, and no later than 90 days after entering into the lease, a written notice about the absence of a disclosure statement.

- In Victoria the tenant may then withhold rent until the disclosure statement is given. The tenant is not liable for rent from the day on which the tenant gave notice until the day the disclosure is given.

- The tenant may terminate the lease by written notice within 7 days after receiving the disclosure notice.

- If the premises are not available for handover on the date specified in the disclosure statement, the tenant is not liable to pay for any rent charged prior to that date.

- If any information in the disclosure statement is misleading, false or materially incomplete, or the tenant has not been given a copy of the proposed lease, then the tenant may give the landlord or his agent written notice of termination of the lease within 28 days after receiving the disclosure statement, (or the tenant being given a copy of the proposed lease, or the date the lease is entered into whichever is the latter.)

- The landlord still has the right to object to the termination of a lease on the grounds that he acted honestly and reasonably and ought to be excused for the contravention provided that the tenant is substantially in as good a position as he would have been, if there was no contravention.

- If the lease requires the tenant to pay or contribute towards the cost of a fit-out, this provision is void if that liability was not disclosed in the disclosure statement. This is particularly relevant in the case of category one works that the landlord usually undertakes, but is paid for by the tenant.

- If on assignment of the lease the tenant asks the landlord to give him a current disclosure statement from a specified date (that is within 3 months before the statement is given). This may mean that the landlord or his agent needs to prepare a new uniform disclosure statement. The landlord or agent can still recover reasonable legal and other costs in connection with the assignment of the lease or sub lease.

- Even though you will notice that the new disclosure statement in section 14.2 allows for an outgoing under the heading of "Sinking Fund for Repairs and Maintenance," the Victorian Act provides that "a provision in a retail lease is void to the extent that it requires the tenant to make a contribution to a sinking fund for capital works".

- The Acts in the other states do allow for the creation of a "sinking fund" for future capital works that can be recovered from the tenant as an outgoing.

- If the retailer's store is in a shopping centre, the retailer must be aware of the way the Act defines a shopping centre as the new statement requires additional information to be given in this case.. For example in Victoria, the Act provides that a retail shopping centre is defined as a cluster of premises that has <u>all</u> of these attributes:-

At least 5 of the premises are retail premises.

The premises are owned by the same person or have (or would have if leased) the same landlord or head landlord.

The premises are located in a single building or in 2 or more buildings that are adjoining, or separated only by common areas, or other areas belonging to the owner of the retail premises or separated only by a road.

The cluster of premises is promoted as or generally regarded as constituting a shopping centre, shopping mall, shopping court or shopping arcade

The essential issues and specific items a new retailer should look for in the disclosure statement

The new disclosure statement has several important and detailed changes that are worth noting, namely:

1. Structures, fixtures, plant and equipment

Whereas the old Part 3, required the landlord to set out structure, fixtures, plant equipment and services to or in the premises provided by the tenant which may or may not have been completed fully by the landlord or his agent, the new disclosure statement sets out a list of 22 items which are required to be highlighted as being provided in the premises.

2. Services and facilities

In addition there is a new section 1.5 that requires disclosure of services and facilities for the benefit of the premises, for example security services, cleaning and so on.

3. Lawful planning area

Section 2.1. describing the permitted use, is the same as Part 5. Section B of the old statement except that it comes with a warning to the tenant that he should investigate whether the proposed use of the premises is lawful under relevant planning laws.

4. Right to sell goods and services

While the old lease allows the tenant to have the right to sell specific goods and services, the new disclosure statement in section 2.2 requires the landlord to answer "yes or no" as to whether the whole of the permitted use is exclusive to the tenant or not.

5. Car Parks

Whereas previously, the landlord had to show the total number of car parks in the centre and the number of car parking bays available for the tenant's exclusive use, the landlord now has to show the number of available spaces for customer parking.

6. Head Leases

Section 4 is new and requires the landlord to state "yes/no", whether the premises are leases under a head lease or crown lease. If the answer is yes, the next question is whether the landlord has provided a copy of the head lease or crown lease to the tenant. In addition, section 4.1 requires the landlord to state the current term of such a lease and whether there is an option to renew the lease and during which period the options will be available

Section 4.4 requires a disclosure by the landlord as to whether or not the head landlord's consent is required to the proposed lease to be entered into between landlord and tenant.

7. Survey Plan

It is no longer necessary for a survey plan to be annexed to the disclosure statement.

8. Handover Date

In section 7.1 the handover date (actual or estimated) must be shown if it is different from the date the lease commences.

9. Tenant's Works

Whereas the old disclosure statement provided for only a list of the tenant's works to be performed by the tenant at its cost before the commencement date of the lease and during the lease term, the new disclosure statement now requires in section 8.1 a description of works to be carried out by the landlord before the lease commences.

- Section 8.2 requires the landlord to provide an estimate of the expected contribution by the tenant towards the cost of the landlord's works as well as the costs in relation to any maintenance and repair outgoings that have been included in the schedule of outgoings.

- Whilst not required previously, now the landlord has to also state whether he has requirements about the quality and standard of the shop front and fit-out. This may be by way of a fit-out guide.

10. Requirement to provide turnover

Now the landlord must state whether the tenant is required to provide details of turnover.

11. Non recovery of specific outgoings from the tenant

Now there is a note in the disclosure statement informing the tenant that according to section 50 of the Victorian Act, the landlord may be prevented from claiming certain costs such as recovery of land tax. Also under section 52 of the Victorian Act, the landlord may also be prevented from claiming costs for certain repairs and maintenance.

In addition section 41 of the Victorian Act prevents the landlord from claiming any capital costs of the building in which the premises are located. This is not the case in the other state Acts.

12. Renovation and Redevelopment of the Centre

Whereas previously, the landlord merely had to state whether planning approval for renovations, redevelopments or the extension of the centre had been obtained, now the landlord or his agent must state whether at that point in time any alterations works are planned, to the premises or building/centre including surrounding roads during the term of the lease or any other further term.

13. Relocation of tenant

The new statement now requires the landlord or his agent to state the clause number in the lease that deals with the relocation of the tenant and with the demolition of the premises or centre/building where applicable.

14. Trading Hours

Landlords must now provide the core trading hours specifically relevant to the tenant (not the shopping centre/building) on a day by day basis including trading on public holidays. Therefore, if a trader such as a pharmacist, gym or video shop, works outside the normal centre hours, this must now be stated.

This raises the question as to whether the tenants trading hours, if agreed upon, will not be subject to a late night trading charge for hours worked outside normal centre trading hours.

There is a further clause which provides for whether the tenant is permitted access to the premises and centre/building outside trading hours, for example bakeries or butcher shops and the like.

15. Disclosure of centre turnover information and number of shops

Whereas previously, the landlord had to reveal the number of retail premises in the Centre, the new statement requires the landlord to state the number of shops.

The new disclosure statement requires the disclosure of annual turnover figures of the centre for the previous accounting period, if collected by the lessor. The turnover will have to be declared on either a GST inclusive or GST exclusive basis, which may differ from what is often declared in shopping centre reports. This will again give tenants access to confidential information and may cause some problems in negotiation, particularly if figures show a downward trend.

The new disclosure statement requires the disclosure of information for speciality shops (in no less than three identified categories namely food, non-food and services) for the previous accounting period and on a per square metre basis. Again the information must be provided if collected by the landlord.

16. Expiry date of leases of tenants greater than 1000 square meters

The new section 23 of the statement requires the disclosure of the expiry date of leases of tenants of more than 1000 square meters. Although not contentious, the person completing the disclosure statement must ensure that that the expiry dates of such tenants is absolutely accurate. Any error could lead to a claim for misleading and deceptive conduct.

17. Tenancy Mix

Under new section 24, the floor plan to be provided now must in addition to showing the tenancy mix as previously, also show common area, trading, kiosks and major tenants.

In the case of competitors, the old assurance by the landlord that the centre "is an ongoing entity and changes will take place from time to time" is no longer relevant in the new statement. The landlord must answer" yes or no" as to whether he assures the tenant that the current tenant mix will not be altered by the introduction of a competitor. To comply with this, landlords may have to undertake some extensive research on each category in a centre to ascertain the impact an additional tenant will have on the category.

18. Traffic Flow

In the new statement, details of the customer traffic flow are still required together with an attached schedule showing this. The traffic flow over a number of years may also be shown. The new statement may require lessors to ensure that the equipment used to measure traffic flows is carefully tested and monitored for accuracy. If there are inaccuracies, then the lessor will need to have tried his best to ensure that the equipment has been properly tested.

19. Casual Mall Leasing

If the centre adheres to the casual mall leasing code of practice as determined by the Shopping Centre Council, a copy of the casual mall policy must now be included with the disclosure statement.

20. Current legal proceedings

Section 27 of the new disclosure statement has a new requirement to disclose details of any current legal proceedings in relation to the lawful use of the premises or building/centre. However, there is no definition of either the term "lawful use" or "current legal proceedings." To comply with this section, the landlord or agent will have to provide a list of any proceedings that is ongoing between the landlord and any tenant in that centre or complex. Besides affecting the confidentiality of discussions between landlord and tenant, disputes may include claims for arrear rent or spurious disputes by a tenant.

The disclosure of such information to a new or existing tenant may affect the future relationship between the landlord and the tenant.

21. Representations during negotiations

There is now a new section 28 that must be completed dealing with any oral or written representations made by a landlord or agent during negotiations.

22. Acknowledgement of receipt of disclosure statement

Section 31 requires an acknowledgement by the tenant that he has received the disclosure statement. In the two states of New South Wales and Queensland, we previously had a lessee's disclosure statement which was not applicable in Victoria. We now have uniformity in all three states

Checklist and warning for tenants

The statement now comes with a warning and a checklist for all tenants who should consider nine key questions before signing the document namely:

1. Does the planning authority allow your proposed use for the premises under planning law?

2. Is the security of your occupancy affected by

   (a)Mortgage charges or encumbrances granted by the landlord?

   (b)Rights and obligations under a head lease?

3. Do the premises comply with building and safety regulations? Are the premises affected by outstanding notices by any authority?

4. Could your trading be affected by disturbances or changes to the building or centre?

5. Does the landlord require you to refurbish the premises regularly or at the end of the lease?

6. Can the landlord end the lease early even if you comply with the lease?

7. Are all the existing structures, fixtures and plant and equipment in good working order?

8. Are you required to make good the premises at the end of the lease?

9. Is the tenancy mix of the shopping centre (if applicable) likely to change during the term of the lease?

Failure by the landlord or his agent to have answers to all these questions may give the tenant second thoughts about entering into the lease.

1. Attachments

If applicable the following attachments must be included with the disclosure statement:

- Plan of premises

- The head lease or Crown Lease

- Any additional attachments

If the premises are in a retail shopping centre the following additional attachments must be included if applicable:-

- A Floor Plan

- Customer traffic flow statistics

- A casual mall licensing policy

- Any additional attachments

Checking the disclosure statement after the deal has been negotiated

Frequently the retailer is required to check the disclosure statement after the deal has been concluded.

The details as contained in the statement continue to be considered factual throughout the term of the lease and throughout the term of any renewal and to options contained in the original lease. If any of the representations are misleading, the tenant may recover damages.

It can't be emphasised enough that you should insist on all details and representations given to you by the landlord or his representative during the negotiation phase, be included in the disclosure statement. In particular check all the correspondence carefully. Often concessions obtained early in the lease negotiations are not carried forward in later letters. Be aware that concessions won from the same landlord in other lease negotiations should be transferred to the current lease. Insist that they be included in the new disclosure statement and are carried forward to the lease.

If you are having the lease checked by you solicitor or consultant, ask him to check to ensure that the provisions of the disclosure statement have been carried forward to the final lease terms.

8

Making a lease offer

When negotiating a lease with a landlord, the best approach a retailer can take is to acknowledge receipt of the landlord's lease offer while preparing their own lease offer in advance. In this way, when there are further talks, instead of attempting to bargain down the landlord's offer the retailer's lease offer will become the basis of the discussions. The landlord is then placed in a position of trying to negotiate up from the retailer's offer.

In addition the lease offer will be a check list for the retailer to ensure that all aspects of the negotiation have been covered.

A standard letter of offer for shopping centre tenancies

This letter has been prepared for a pharmacy tenant but can be adapted for any retailer depending on the circumstances of negotiation

Project Leasing Manager
Happiness Shopping Centre
P.O. Box
Melbourne
Victoria

Dear Sir/Madam

Re: Lease XYZ RETAIL STORE – Shop 12 - Happiness Shopping Centre

Thank you for your letter of invitation of 10 July 2014. We have now visited the centre and have reviewed the indicative plan which you have presented to us.

As such we would be willing to put the following proposal for consideration to our board:

PROPOSAL	
Location:	Shop 1 lower ground floor
Lessee:	Partners as per current pharmacy practice as of this date or a management company to be nominated
Size:	200 square meters (subject to survey) Irrespective of the surveyed size of the premises. Premises, the rental in year one will not be more than the agreed amount.
Handover date:	Approximately 4 October 2014
Lease term:	5 Years and 3 months commencing 28 days after hand-over of the premises or commencement of trading from the store whichever is the later in a clean shell state condition. We require the extra three months in order to allow us to trade through an additional Christmas.
Option period:	5 Years. No restrictions will be accepted on the lessor exercising such option.
Base rent:	$xxxxx for year 1 plus GST. However, we will only pay 75% of the base rental until the following has been completed by the lessor.

	• All stores are open and trading .
	• All car parks are open and available for customers.
	• All the lessors works have been completed.
	• The supermarket is open and trading.
Rent reviews:	4%. Fixed for the term of the lease. Unless the parties have agreed to a new rental, a market review will be conducted on the exercise of the option in accordance with the Retail Tenancy Act. During the option period rent will again increase at the rate of 4% annually from the start of the second year of such an option period.
Outgoings:	As applicable to our tenancy (exclusive of carbon tax).
Promotion levy:	3% of base rental.
Opening promotion:	$1000 payable 14 days prior to commencement of trading.
Guarantor:	The directors of the Company.
Bank Guarantee:	The equivalent of 2 months base rental excluding GST.
Percentage Rental:	Pharmacists are legally required not to share their income with anyone who is not a pharmacist. Therefore percentage rent will not be applicable in the lease. However for planning purposes the lessee will undertake to provide, monthly sales figures comprising front of shop sales plus NHS income.

Legal Costs:	Each party will be expected to bear its own legal costs in respect of the lease preparation, or any ancillary documents or guarantees. The lessee will be responsible for the costs of registering the Lease.
The Act applicable to Lease:	The current Retail Leases Act in the applicable state.
Exclusivity:	A special provision is required as follows: that no more than one tenancy will be permitted to dispense pharmaceutical products (as provided for under the National Health Scheme) at the centre during the lease term and option period. In the event of the redevelopment of the centre of more than 100 retail tenancies allowing for an additional pharmacy being permitted in the centre, then the lessee shall be entitled to the last right of refusal on the lease for such tenancy. OR If no exclusivity has been promised, in the event of a second pharmacy opening in the centre, our rental will be permanently reduced to 75% of the rental payable at that time.
Payments:	All rental, outgoings and promotion contributions to be payable monthly by way of EFT only. No direct debits will be acceptable.
Lessor contribution:	$xxxxx contribution is payable 7 days after presentation of invoice (including GST). Repayment of the contribution in the event of assignment of the lease will be as per your lease offer. However, if the approved assignee is prepared to accept the liability then no repayment will be required by the pharmacist.

Fit-out:	We will supply our normal set of plans/ drawings for approval at no cost prior to proceeding with the shop fit-out. Signage package will be provided for approval. Consulting, design, survey costs or other engineering costs will payable by the lessee will be capped at $X. There will be no charge for hoardings.
Kiosks:	Whilst we accept kiosks as part of a centre layout, no kiosks will be erected within 10 meters of our lease line which will affect the sightline of the premises.
Rent in Advance:	The one month's rental to be paid on the signing of the lease which will be applied to the first month's rent when payable.
Pub Liab. Insurance	$20m
Retail Category Classification:	Pharmacy
Permitted use:	The operation of a pharmacy and health food shop including retail sales and services and the operation of a mini lab as well as other goods and services as normally undertaken by a pharmacist as determined from time to time, (such as sales of confectionary, sporting and disability aids, health shoes, wheelchairs as well as the operation of a beauty parlour or perfumery). The premises will also be used from time to time for the operation of medical and para-medical service providers and special medicine preparations.

Solicitor:	This offer would naturally be subject to our solicitor sighting and approving the disclosure statement and lease and its terms.
Lessors works:	The premises will have sprinklers and air conditioned to a quality in accordance with the Australian air conditioning standard. The landlord shall guarantee that the premises shall be water and weather sealed at the time of entering into the lease.
Lease terms:	All amendments to standard leases previously negotiated to be carried forward to the lease for this centre.
Painting:	We will undertake to paint and restore the store not at fixed intervals, but as and when necessary by mutual agreement during the lease term.
Electricity:	In the event of electricity charged to us as a result of bulk buying by the lessor, the tariff charged to us will be the "best tariff "rate applicable and in accordance with current electricity regulations. The pharmacist will be able to use its own electricity provider if it is more cost effective.
Binding agreement:	There will be no binding agreement between the lessor and the lessee to enter into a lease, until the necessary legal documentation is drawn up and executed by all parties.

Storeroom:	In the event of a storeroom being supplied, as part of the agreement, we require a licence agreement be supplied for such storeroom to run concurrently with the lease and to terminate at the same time as the lease. No outgoings will be applicable for the storeroom.
Outposts:	The landlord shall permit us to have two outposts per annum in the centre mall at the commercial rate. The timing of such outposts shall be by mutual agreement.
Relocation:	Relocation of our pharmacy during the lease or option terms as a result of the total re-development of the centre, will be permitted once the heath commission has approved such relocation and the landlord agrees to compensate us and pay for all costs of relocation, erection and fit-out of such new pharmacy as provided under the Act.
Deregulation:	In the event of the deregulation of the pharmacy industry, allowing supermarkets and other retail chains to incorporate pharmacies within their stores, the lessee shall be permitted to either surrender the lease or renegotiate at the time the terms and conditions of the balance of the lease with the lessor.
Should the above proposal be acceptable to the lessor, we would be happy to submit an amended formal lease invitation to our board of directors for approval.	

The document will need to be signed and dated.

Some Additional Terms That Could Be Included In Lease Offers

Quite often the parties believe that they have agreed to the commercial terms of the lease but then find that when they receive the landlord's standard lease documents there are terms and conditions contained therein which are simply not acceptable to the retailer.

To overcome this, retailers have started to put the following special conditions in their lease offers. In any event, when checking the lease you should request that such clauses be deleted or amended. (Some of these provisions have already been dealt with previously).

Kiosks: No Kiosk (other than existing Kiosks) will be permitted within 10 meters of our lease line which will affect the view of our store or impair ingress or egress from our store.

Directors Guarantees: In the event that the retail store is a company no director's a guarantee or bank guarantees will be provided by the lessee.

Method of Payment of Rent: The payment of rent and outgoings will be. by electronic transfer and not by direct debit.

Opening Promotion Levy: If the tenancy is to be in a new shopping centre and there is to be a "once off" opening promotion levy, this levy must be payable 14 days before the commencement of trading from the store. In addition the lessor will provide details within 3 months of opening on how the opening promotion contributions have been spent.

Consulting Fees: The retailer will not be responsible for the payment of any consulting, plan approval or engineering costs in respect of the fit-out.

CPI Rent Increases: If rent increases are to be on the basis of CPI plus a fixed percentage which is permitted in all states except Victoria, we require a provision that if CPI is negative that rent will fall on the anniversary date of the lease.

Outgoings: If we do a deal based on net rent plus outgoings and the deal is say for less than 1 year (which in some states would take us outside the Act), irrespective of whether we fall under the Act, we must make the following lease provision:

- In the case of stores in Queensland, South Australia and Victoria, land tax is not recoverable as an outgoing from tenants.

- In the case of West Australia management fees are not recoverable as an outgoing from tenants.

- In the case of Victoria management fees may not increase by more than CPI annually

Tenancies in Strip Centres: If the retailer is opening a retail store in a strip centre that may be subject to flooding from storms, we must provide that the lease contains a condition requiring the landlord to agree that on the handover of the premises to the tenant that the premises are water and weather sealed.

Insurance: The following provisions should be included:

- Public liability insurance will be taken out to an amount of $20m and in addition the retailer will only keep an industrial special risks policy.

- The company's insurance policies are to be in the name of the retailer and only the lessor's interest will be noted in the policy.

- No policy will be taken out by the lessee in respect of limitation of the landlord's liability in the event of a claim.

Fit-out Contributions: If you have negotiated an incentive deal with the landlord who may have contributed to the fit-out, the following provision in the lease is required; that the fittings making up the contribution will remain the property of the landlord for the term of the lease but the retailer may or may not remove it at the end of the lease term. The taxation implications of this type of incentive are very complicated and you should first clear this with your tax adviser.

In the case of a fit-out contribution which includes a "claw back" provision, there must be a provision in the lease stating that in the event of a relocation to an assignee acceptable to the lessor, no repayment of the fit-out contribution will be required by the tenant retailer provided that the assignee is prepared to accept this contingent liability.

Cost of Hoardings during Fit-Out: All costs of hoardings during the fit-out store will be payable by the lessor.

Painting and Restoration during the lease term: Painting and restoring of the premises during the lease term and option periods will occur as and when necessary by mutual consent and not as decided by the landlord unilaterally.

Quality of Air Conditioning to be provided: You must request a provision in the lease to ensure that *"The lessor shall provide air conditioning to the premises of a quality so as to provide comfort conditions even when the lighting heat intensity exceeds 50 watts per square metre of the floor area of the demised premises including other heat producing equipment within the premises"*. This is in accordance with the Australian standard.

Fire walls sprinklers and emergency lighting: We require a provision in the lease or confirmation from the landlord that irrespective of these costs being included in the definition of outgoings in the lease, that the landlord agrees to ensure the following:

• That the landlord will conducts a six monthly inspection of the fire walls and these will be tagged to this effect.

- That the landlord will conduct a 3 monthly inspection to check that the pressure to the sprinklers in your tenancy is correct and that they will function in the event of an emergency.

- All fire hydrants hoses and reels within the common area of the centre are also checked at least every 3 months to ensure than the equipment has not been vandalised and will work in an emergency.

Change of signs and colour: We require a general provision that no permission will be required from the lessor in the event of a total change of corporate colour or image change of the entire network.

Restoration of shop-front during lease term: There should be provision in the lease that this will only be required as and when necessary if mutually agreed to by both parties.

Services: In the event of electricity or gas being provided by the lessor to the premises, this will be charged at the same tariff rate as paid by the landlord or at the best rate. In addition, the retailer will be able to acquire such services from their own providers.

Relocation: A section of the lease offer must include the following:

- That the alternative premises offered will be in a position in the centre which in no worse than the position the lessee currently enjoys.

- The rental will be the same rental as the current lease adjusted to take into account the commercial value of the new premises at the time of relocation as agreed by the parties, or in the absence of agreement, as determined by a valuer appointed by the Small Business Commissioner.

- The lessor will in addition, agree to waive the "making good" and decommissioning costs of the existing premises and pay for any surrender of lease legal costs.

Market Reviews in Victoria: In Victoria, if there is to be market review on an exercise of the option in the lease; ensure that there is a provision in the lease for the market review to be completed first before you have to exercise your option. Other States have the timetable the right way around (namely that we have the review first, then the right to exercise the option). This is not the case in Victorian legislation.

Lease Term: Should the date of commencement of trading be delayed as a result of the late handover of the premises prior to fit-out, then the commencement date and the termination date will be adjusted accordingly.

Storeroom: In the event of a storeroom being supplied as part of the rental, request a licence agreement to be supplied for such storeroom to run concurrently with the lease and to terminate at the same time as the lease.

New Shopping Centres:

Gross rental for the new tenancy will be limited to a percentage of sales until such time as the centre is completed. The centre shall be deemed to be completed when all the following have occurred

•   All majors are trading

•   Car parking is 100% complete

•   95% of the specialty areas are trading or malls to be substantially complete

9

Purchasing a new store and taking over an assignment of the lease from an existing tenant or assigning a lease to a new operator

When a retailer takes over a store from another tenant or the retailer plans to sell a store to another retailer, his understanding of the lease implications, are essential.

It is therefore imperative that when you are thinking about a possible sale of your business that you insure that your "lease is in order". Remember that the lease is one of the key pillars on which your negotiations with the purchaser, is based. The quality of the lease could either break or make your sale.

What should the seller take into account?

There are two major considerations for a retailer to take into account:

1.   Do I have a good retail lease that will ensure I can maximize its value in the event of a sale of the retail store?

2.   What is my position when the lease is up for renewal but it contains no further option?

•   Note that at present it would be difficult for the landlord to accept a higher rental from another retailer and simply evict you.

- If for instance, you are a pharmacist, under the Guild/ Government agreement you may have some protection preventing another pharmacy taking up your vacated space. It is important in your lease negotiation that you are aware of this.

- If you loose you premises you may still be able to save the value of your goodwill by relocating outside the shopping centre to a strip centre. However the ability to achieve this is hard to predict and each case will be different.

What will a buyer be looking at in the lease when carrying out a due diligence on the purchase of your store?

In arriving at the final selling price it would be prudent for a potential buyer to carry out a proper due diligence on the lease underpinning the purchase of the store. There may well be a number of provisions contained in the lease that have to be taken into account in the final purchase price

These include:

- Does the lease provide for a refit of the premises at the end of the current lease term? If it does the purchaser may have to spend $100,000 to $1,500,000 of his own funds within a short while of taking over the store. This may mean that an appropriate sum of money may have to be deducted from the purchase price.

- Given the flat retail conditions in some shopping centres, the store may have been enjoying a marketing or rental abatement of about $2500 per month being credited to the monthly statement. This will mean that the rental paid as per the profit and loss presented could be understated. (Often these rental abatements will cease on assignment). Such credits should be added back and deducted from the profit of the business.

- Many leases provide for the painting of the premises every 3 years. This may well cost up to $5000 for each painting. If the date for painting has not yet been reached before the takeover, a sum equivalent to the above should be taken into account in the purchase price.

- If you are buying a store in a rising rental market, and the lease calls for a market review, which is to take place after the new buyer has taken over, the purchaser may well have to ask for an independent valuer's opinion of what this may well be. A substantial increase in the market rental will affect the future profitability of the business and should be taken into account when determining the profitability on which a return on investment will be calculated.

Leases often provide for several months rental payment into the centre's promotion fund on the assignment of the lease. Who is to pay this assignment fee needs to be negotiated by the parties.

In addition, some leases provide that on assignment of the lease there is to be an automatic market review. Again you should ensure that you obtain an independent valuer's opinion of what this is likely to be. This should be taken into account in determining the profitability of the business.

It is important to ascertain the "vintage" of the lease. If the lease is old and is currently in the second option period, you may well be stuck with all the old provisions of the various State Acts. This could be disadvantageous to a new buyer .It may well be a negotiating point for the buyer to rather negotiate a new lease than live with a "bad old lease"

If the business is in an old centre that is likely to be refurbished or upgraded shortly, there may be certain outgoings such as building maintenance, or air conditioning being upgraded, or a new centre owner substantially increasing management costs. These factors could cause an increase in future outgoings costs. You need to take this into account in assessing the realistic future occupancy costs of the store.

All leases provide for a" make good provision" at the end of the lease. If the store has been restructured to suit the needs of the current occupier, it may well cost a substantial amount to put the store back to its original condition.

If possible, always request whether there were photos of the store at the date of hand over. Comparing old and current photos, will allow the purchaser to ascertain what the potential liability will be for making good at the end of the lease.

New legislation in some states requires the person assigning the lease to provide a new disclosure statement on the centre. Make sure that you ask for this, as it will provide you with details of any future developments of the centre that may result in some disruption to trading while this redevelopment takes place.

If there is an "exclusivity provision" in the lease as to the number of similar businesses that may operate in a centre, make sure that this provision continues on assignment of the lease.

10

The rights of franchisees and franchisors under the State Retail Leases Acts

In Australia the franchisee and the franchisor both have rights and obligations under State as well as Federal legislation. In this chapter, we will look at their State rights, and in the following chapter their Federal rights (that contains the latest amendments to Federal Legislation that came into effect on the 1st of January 2015).

State Legislation – Victoria

Victoria is the most progressive of all the states in its dealings with retail tenancy legislation and the way in which it affects landlords, franchisees and franchisors.

Summary of the Victorian franchise legislation

The material in this chapter does not quote the act in its entirety. However the following points summarize a franchisees position:

- The provisions of the Act apply in the case of the franchisor entering into a lease with the landlord for premises after 1 May 2003.

- Franchisors as part of the franchising process normally enter into a single unit franchise occupancy licence agreement. This allows the franchisee to occupy the premises leased by the franchisor from the landlord for the purpose of establishing and conducting the franchise operation.

- The franchisor normally requires the franchisee to pay the landlord the rent, outgoings, security deposit and any other requirement of the lease.

- The franchisee is also obligated to observe all the covenants of the lease imposed on the franchisor.

- The franchisee must acknowledge that the terms of the lease will be adhered to as if it were the lessee.

- The franchisee acknowledges that where there is any inconsistency between the lease and the licence agreement the lease will prevail.

- The franchisee agrees to have read the lease and is familiar with its terms

These details may at times seem unnecessary reading or time consuming but as always in negotiations, it is necessary to understand the "small print".

The arrangements between the franchisor, franchisee and landlord are affected by the inclusion of the new provisions in the Victorian Act in the following way:

1. **Under the act the landlord may reserve the right to refuse a sub lease or mortgage**

   Section 63 of the new Act stipulates that a retail premises lease may contain a provision allowing the landlord the absolute discretion to refuse to consent to the following:

   The granting of a sub-lease, licence or concession in respect of all or part of the retail premises.

The parting with occupancy rights to all or part of the premises.

The franchisor mortgaging or otherwise encumbering the franchisor's estate or interest in the lease. This last provision, if it becomes general practice, may make it impossible for franchisors to grant franchises. It may also hamper the franchisee's ability to finance their fit-outs by a mortgage of the lease.

Franchisors, who propose to establish a franchise in premises where franchisees may use the lease as security for finance, are best off negotiating the terms in their leases to enable them to manage the franchise.

Section 63 allows the landlord to become an active party to the franchise occupancy licence arrangement, both as to the vetting of the agreement and charging of a fee for this involvement.

2. Key money and goodwill payments prohibited

Section 23 of the Act provides that "key-money" is prohibited .Any form of payment by a retailer to a landlord or any consideration for the goodwill of any business carried on in the premises is forbidden.

However, various other payments, that do not constitute rent, but are valid, are also set out in this section; These include rent in advance, bonds, security deposits and guarantees .They even include, seeking and accepting payment for the grant of a franchise in connection with the lease being granted.

Even more important from a franchising point of view, section 23(3) specifically provides that the landlord may recover reasonably incurred costs from the retailer incurred in investigating a proposed assignee of the lease or sub lessee of the premises (which the licence agreement confers)

Under the state Act both the licence agreement and details of the franchisee in now permitted to be vetted by the landlord.

There appears to be no limit to the amount that can be recovered beyond what is reasonable. Since legal costs are no longer recoverable from retailers under the Act in Victoria, this cost may be a way of recovering, these expenses.

3. Disclosure statements between franchisor and franchisee

If a franchisor proposes to grant a licence to a person to use all or part of the retail premises, wholly or predominately for the carrying on of the business under a name or identifying mark, commonly associated with or controlled by the retailer or a person or corporation connected with the franchisor, then the franchisor must supply the proposed licensee *within 7 days before* the grant of the licence. The following procedures must be followed:

1. A copy of the disclosure statement must be given to the franchisee concerning the lease. Failure to provide a disclosure statement may attract a penalty of $1000 or 10 penalty points.

2. As the disclosure statement has been given to the franchisee, any changes that the franchisor is aware of or could reasonably be expected to be aware of that may have affected the information in the disclosure statement must now be disclosed to the franchisee.

3. It is therefore essential that the occupancy licence agreement contains a provision that the "franchisee acknowledges that he or she has received the disclosure statement within 7 days of signing of the licence agreement".

4. The franchisor will most likely need to receive a new disclosure document from the landlord to give to the

franchisee. Sufficient time needs to be allowed for receipt of the disclosure statement from the landlord.

5. The franchisor must make a decision as to whether he wishes to have the franchisee under the Act or not. If not, this may be in conflict with the franchising code.

6. If the lease is entered into between the landlord and the franchisee, the lease will automatically apply to the franchisee as if he were the tenant.

7. If the lease is entered into between the franchisor and the landlord and the franchisor enters into a licence agreement with the franchisee, such a licence agreement will now have to be approved by the landlord.

8. Disputes between the franchisor and the franchisee in relation to the premises will be treated as part of the overall franchising relationship. They will be subject to the provisions under the Trade Practices Act.

9. This is a complicated section in the act and needs to be fully understood by any person acting on behalf of either for the franchisee or the franchisor.

South Australia and West Australia

The states of South Australia and West Australia have recently introduced franchising bills to examine the State regulation of franchising. Franchisees contemplating the purchase of a franchise in these states need to check the progress of these bills before signing any documents.

11

The rights of franchisees and franchisors under the Federal Franchising Code of Conduct

Federal Legislation:

The federal legislation governing franchising is contained in an act known as the Competition and Consumer (Industry Codes- Franchising) Regulations 2014. Select Legislative Instrument No 168 2014.

Every franchisee or proposed franchisee needs to obtain a copy of the Code either from the franchisor or from the Office of Drafting and Publishing Attorney-General's department Canberra.

The old regulations and Code have been substantially overhauled and a new franchising code of conduct has now been enacted by Parliament which is to take effect from 1 January 2015. (There are however some transitional provisions relating to disclosure documents and the application of some clauses which overlap with the old legislation).

I do not intend to present all the details contained in the Code. This should be read in detail by any proposed franchisee, however, I have highlighted the main points, that franchisees need be aware of prior to entering into negotiations.

What documents are required to cover a franchise arrangement?

The fundamental documents in any franchise arrangement are as follows:

• A copy of the franchise agreement, in the form it is to be executed.

• A disclosure statement.

• A copy of the code.

The disclosure statement must be given at least 14 days before the franchisee either enters into the franchise agreement or pays any non-refundable money in advance to the franchisor or his agent or associate.

The franchise disclosure statement must be given to a franchisee if the franchisee is proposing to renew or extend the term of the franchise agreement.

If the franchisee makes a written request for a disclosure statement, the franchisor must provide the franchisee with a current disclosure statement within 14 days of the request. Remember that a franchisee can request a disclosure statement only once in any 12 month period

What are the fundamental conditions of a franchise agreement?

The Code prescribes the following specific conditions that must be included in all franchise agreements:

Cooling off period:

• A prospective franchisee is entitled to a cooling off period of seven days after entering into a franchise agreement (this is not the case of a renewal extension or transfer of the franchise) or in making any payment under the agreement whichever occurs earlier.

- If the franchisee terminates the agreement during the cooling off period he is entitled to a refund of all payments less any reasonable franchisor's expenses (which must be described fully in the agreement) within 14 days.

Membership of franchise associations

- The franchisor is prohibited from preventing franchisees forming an association with other prospective franchisees for a lawful purpose. However, it is unlawful for franchisees to meet to make a contract or arrangement or arrive at an understanding for the purpose of fixing, controlling or maintaining the price that they will charge for goods and services.

General release from liabilities

- A clause which prohibits the inclusions of any general "release from liabilities" by the franchisor or the release of waivers of representations" that is given to the franchisee by the franchisors during negotiations is not acceptable.

Franchisees right to transfer or novate a franchise agreement

- A franchisee has the right at all times to transfer or novate a franchise agreement. This request must be in writing and the franchisor may not unreasonably withhold consent.

- The franchisor can only withhold consent in the following circumstances:

  1. If the transferee is unlikely to meet the financial obligations of the agreement.

  2. If the transferee does not meet a particular requirement of the agreement.

3. If the transferee does not meet the franchisors selection criteria.

4. If the transfer will have an adverse effect on the franchise system in general.

5. If the transferee does not agree in writing to comply with the obligations under the franchise agreement.

6. If the franchisee has breached the franchise agreement and has not remedied the breach.

- Franchisors will under the new regulations, be able to request certain information from an existing or current franchisee before they agree to transfer or novation of the franchise agreement .The franchisee is deemed to have consented to the transfer or novation if he does not object to the transfer within 42 days of the written notice.

- Whilst the franchisor has the right to exercise his discretion in objecting to a transfer or novation, he may not be permitted to act unconscionably in the exercise of his discretion.

Renewal of the agreement when it expires

- The franchisor is not obliged to renew the franchise agreement when it expires, unless there is an option for a further period and the franchisee exercises the option as per the requirements of the agreement.

- If the agreement runs for more than 6 months, the franchisor must notify the franchisee at least 6 months before the end of the term of the franchise agreement as to whether it will be renewed or not. If it is to be renewed, the franchisee must then enter into a new agreement with the franchisee.

- If the agreement has been made for less than 6 months then 1 months' notice is required.

Termination of the franchise agreement

- The franchising Code sets out specific requirements where parties seek to terminate a franchise agreement. These essentially cover 3 circumstances:-

    1. Where the franchisee has breached the franchise agreement.

    2. If special circumstances apply in the Code that permits the franchisor to terminate the agreement.

    3. Where the franchisee has not breached the agreement, but the franchisor seeks to terminate the agreement in accordance with its terms but without the consent of the franchisee to its termination

- In the first case where the franchisee seeks to terminate the agreement due to the breach of the agreement, the franchisor must give the franchisee 30 days' notice in writing, of his intention to terminate the agreement. The franchisor must stipulate exactly what needs to be done to remedy the breach.

- If the breach is remedied within the prescribed time frame, the franchisor can no longer proceed with the termination unless there are special circumstances. These circumstances are listed as follows:

    1. If the franchisee no longer holds a licence required to carry on the franchise. For example in the case of a liquor retail franchise, where the franchisee has lost his liquor licence.

    2. If the franchisee becomes bankrupt or insolvent, puts his affairs under administration or if his company is deregistered by the Australian Securities and Investments Commission.

3. If the franchisee voluntarily abandons the franchise.

4. If the franchisee is convicted of a serious offence.

5. If the franchisee operates the franchise in a way that endangers public health or safety.

6. If the franchisee is fraudulent in connection with the operation of the franchise.

7. If the franchisee and franchisor mutually agree to the termination of the agreement.

- If the franchisor decides to terminate the agreement, without the franchisee's consent, having given proper notice of his intentions, the franchisee has the right to use the dispute resolution procedure as contained in Part 4 of the Code.

- The new Code provides for a statement in the agreement of the franchisee's rights at the end of the term. This includes prescribed wording that must be used depending on whether the franchisee has a right to extend, a right to renew or neither of those rights.

Leases and Licence agreements

Usually the agreement includes a copy of the lease for the premises and or any licence agreements given to the franchisee for the right to occupy the premises.

Sometimes franchise lease arrangements are complicated and tricky. For instance, the lease maybe in the name of the franchisor and the franchisee is expected to be responsible for paying the rent directly to the landlord. He may also be required to give the landlord a "back to back" guarantee in respect of the bank guarantee the franchisor, has given to the landlord in support of the lease. In other cases, the lease is in the name of the franchisee, who is responsible for paying the rent and providing the bank and other guarantees.

Act in Good Faith

The new Code provides that parties to a franchise agreement," must act towards another party with good faith". This obligation applies to any dealing or dispute relating to the agreement as well as the negotiation of the agreement. Franchise agreements cannot limit or exclude this obligation.

A party may be liable for a civil penalty if it breaches this obligation.

Responsibilities before entering into the franchise agreement

This obligation in respect of pre-contractual negotiations and dispute resolution extends the common law position. For both parties it creates a perspective as to what constitutes good faith during negotiations.

Before a franchisor can enter into, renew or receive a non-refundable payment relating to a franchise agreement, the franchisor must obtain a written statement from the prospective franchisee that he has received, read and had a reasonable opportunity to understand the disclosure statement and code.

The franchisor may not enter into a franchise agreement unless he has received a statement signed by the prospective franchisee, confirming that he has been given advice about the proposed franchise agreement by an independent legal adviser, business adviser or accountant or has been told that he should obtain advice from an adviser, and has decided not to seek it.

Marketing and Advertising Fees

The new Code requires franchisors to keep a separate bank account for marketing and advertising fees. The Code expects franchisors to pay the fees on the same basis as other franchisees for franchisor operated stores. The purpose of this amendment to the Code is to increase greater equality in relation to marketing funds.

Post term restraints of trade

Many franchisors, who included in past franchise agreements post-termination restraints, will be greatly affected by the new amendments to the Code. Franchisors will be forced to pay for the protection afforded by such restraints if they decline a franchisee's request to renew their franchise agreement.

As a result of the above amendment any restraint of trade clause in a franchise agreement will not be enforceable in the following situations:

- If the franchisee wishes to have the franchise agreement renewed on similar terms.

- If the franchisee is not in breach of the agreement.

- If the franchisee abides by all the confidentiality clauses in the agreement and does not infringe the intellectual property of the franchisor.

- If the franchisor did not renew the franchise agreement and either the franchisee claimed compensation (but the compensation given was only a nominal amount and did not genuinely compensate the franchisee or the agreement did not allow the franchisee to claim compensation).

Dispute Resolutions

- The Code provides that if either party refers a dispute to a mediator, both the parties must attend the mediation and try to resolve the dispute.

- A party is thought to be attempting to resolve the dispute if they carry out the following actions:

  1. Attend and participate in meetings at reasonable times.

2. At the beginning of the mediation process make their intentions clear as to what they are trying to achieve.

3. Observe any confidentiality agreements.

4. Does not damage the reputation of the franchise system.

- The parties to a dispute are equally liable for the costs of mediation unless they agree otherwise.

- The costs of mediation include the cost of the mediator, room hire and any expert reports that may be required as agreed upon by the parties.

- The new Code also provides for a new dispute framework that will allow for disputes to be dealt with by an internal dispute resolution procedure. This allows parties the flexibility of not having to go to mediation; however either party still have the right to insist on attending a mediation session.

- Franchisors may not include a clause in the franchise agreement that requires mediation or litigation to take place outside the state or territory in which the franchised business is based.

- Franchise agreements under the new Code, cannot include a clause requiring franchisees to pay for any costs of settling any dispute under the agreement.

Franchise Disclosure Statements

What are the main issues covered by the franchise disclosure document?

As indicated above, after the franchise agreement, the disclosure statement is the second most important document in any franchise arrangement between a franchisor and a franchisee.

Information contained in the disclosure statement provides the basis for thoroughly analyzing the potential for a franchise. It establishes, whether the franchisee will have the expertise to run such a business successfully It is also allows the franchisee the opportunity to investigate the franchisor with whom he is about to "get married "to for 5 years or more and to determine whether all the information contained in the statement is truthful and accurate.

Under the new Code franchisors have been given an extended period, until 1 November 2015 during which they can use their existing disclosure statements.

Franchisors will under the new Code, be required to provide the franchisee with a short summary of key risks called an information statement for a prospective franchisee The layout of this statement is included in Annexure 2 of the Code. This statement will have to be provided as soon as practicable after the prospective franchisee formally expresses an interest in acquiring a franchise business.

The following specific points, (including the new amendments) in the disclosure statement needs to be investigated in detail by any proposed franchisee before entering into any agreement:

Compulsory Information in Franchising Disclosure Statements

The following information in terms of the Code must be included in the disclosure statement:

- Details of the number of franchises in operation.

- Information about existing franchises including locations, contact details and when each franchise was started.

- Information about past franchise businesses, including number of businesses transferred, those terminated, bought back or not renewed in last three financial years.

- Details of any litigation involving directors or associates of the franchisor.

- Disclosure of master franchise details.

- Information in relation to online sales. The franchisor must disclose the respective rights of the franchisor and franchisee to conduct and benefit from online sales. This includes any ability or intention of the franchisor to conduct online sales.

- The franchisor must include details about the possibility to renew. If this is not stated the franchisee will be entitled to compensation. The new code, prescribes a specific way of writing to be used in the disclosure statement when there is no right of renewal.

- In the disclosure statement, the new Code requires a full statement about the rights of the franchisee concerning extending, renewing or neither of these rights. The Code prescribes specific wording to be used for this.

- Information about the relevant experience of each officer of the franchise.

- Information about the relevant business experience of each officer of the franchisor.

- The name of the agent to whom payments must be made.

- The financial stability and business reputation of the franchisor.

If not mentioned in the disclosure statement the franchisor must disclose "materially relevant" facts within a reasonable time or not more than 14 days of the franchisor becoming aware of these facts including the following:

1.   A change in the franchisors majority ownership.

2. Details of criminal and civil legal proceedings involving the franchisor.

3. An award in arbitration against the franchisor.

4. Insolvency of the franchisor.

5. The existence and content of undertakings or orders against the franchisor.

- Details about the site and territory

- The franchisor must detail the area occupied in the agreement. This may include a specific shop in a shopping centre or the whole suburb containing the shopping centre. If it was occupied by a previous franchisee, reasons must be given as to why the previous franchisee ceased to operate.

- Details of the exclusivity or non-exclusivity of nominated territory.

- Types of training and other assistance offered to the franchisee.

- Details of franchisees requirements for the supply of goods or services.

- Financial arrangements and future profitability of the franchise.

- The conditions of financing arrangements as offered by the franchisor.

- Earnings information about the franchise based on reasonable grounds.

- Any obligations for the franchise to enter into other agreements such as leases, subleases, hire purchase agreements or security agreements

- Establishment costs of the business.

- Details of intellectual property, including trademarks, patents, designs or copyright.

- Details of any marketing or other cooperative funds controlled by the franchisor

Matters arising from the receipt of the disclosure statement to be considered by the franchisee or to be discussed with his advisors as part of the negotiation

Each point stated previously that refers to the disclosure statement needs to be carefully evaluated in the light of the following practical considerations:

1. The number and experience of existing Franchises

- The number of franchises, provide some measure of stability and experience of the franchisor. A franchisee's risk may be reduced when he selects a franchisor with a large number of franchisees.

- Equally important is the number of franchise operations that have been closed or repurchased by the franchisor. If these are a large number this usually means that there have been problems in the past. The more franchises that have experienced problems the greater is the risk in purchasing a business

- Talk to some of the current franchisees, and in particular past ones who can offer a unique insight into franchisor's behavior and the service provided to franchisees.

- A franchisee should not be afraid to ask other franchisees whether the actual profit they made each year equaled the amount that the franchisor told them to expect.

- The experience of both the management and directors of the franchisor is critical to the competence of the franchisor. The franchisor, should have sufficient experience so that they can add to your business functioning. They should also have knowledge and understanding about the type of business operation they are selling. The length of their experience often indicates stability and a higher potential for franchises to succeed in the future

2.   Health of the Franchising Operation

The potential franchisee should request a copy of a certified financial statement from the franchisor that indicates a financially healthy organization. In addition taking out a Dun and Bradstreet credit report on the franchisor is useful as it could bring to light any ongoing litigation against the franchisor.

3.   Territory covered by the Franchise

A territory may be defined as a suburb, a city or even just a particular shopping centre. Therefore the franchisee should know his exact boundary. It is important that the franchisee has exclusivity to that territory defined in the statement.

4.   Supply of product

- Ascertain whether the franchisee will be offered the right to be supplied with the entire range of products sold by the franchisor. In addition find out whether you can buy product direct from suppliers who are approved by the franchisor.

- Ascertain if you are required to maintain a level of inventory.

- Ascertain whether you have the right to return goods once purchased.

- Inquire from the franchisor if he or his associate will receive a rebate or financial benefit from the supply of goods or services and whether such rebates are shared directly or indirectly with franchisees.

5.   Training

- One of the most important services offered by the franchisor is training. The amount of training that you receive can be critical to your success. .The best training programs will include a combination of classroom training and on the job training. There should be at least a few weeks training for it to be effective.

- There must be a large amount of assistance provided with the startup of the business. This is the most difficult period and requires a great deal of support. There should be continued help offered on a regular basis as well as during any unexpected crises. For example, in the situation where the franchisee takes ill and cannot operate the franchise for some time.

- The franchisee should inquire whether the franchisor will supply a franchise manual setting out how the franchise model and all its operations are to function. The manual should describe how to use it to best settle into the franchise.

6.   Franchise fee and other financial costs

- The franchise fee and the capital costs of establishing the business are the biggest obstacles for most potential franchisees. Once you establish your own net worth discuss with your banker the amount of money you can borrow.

- Determine from the franchisor what assistance he can provide for financing your business. This may include the costs for the franchises fee, equipment, supplies and operating capital. If this is to be in the form of an agreement make sure that you carefully examine the interest rates and loan conditions. Always have the entire document checked out by your financial adviser.

- Determine how long the franchise is expected to operate and if there will be sufficient revenue to cover expenses. This will help you to calculate the amount of funding that you will need to cover this deficit.

- If the franchisee requires a payment before the franchise agreement is entered into, the franchisee should ascertain why the money is required, how the money is to be applied, who will hold the money and the conditions under which a payment will be refunded.

7. Marketing or other cooperative funds

If the franchisee is required to contribute to a marketing fund controlled by the franchisor, the franchisee needs to ask the following questions:

- Who else contributes to the fund, for example the franchisor or an outside supplier?

- How much does the franchisee contribute, and whether other franchisees contribute at a different rate?

- Who controls and administers the fund?

- Is the fund audited? If so, by whom? How can the fund's financial statements be inspected?

- What kind of expenses will the fund be used for?

- Does the fund contribute to the goods and services of the franchisor or its associates?

- Is the franchisor is required to spend part of the funds in advertising or promotion of the franchisee's own business?

Other new amendments to the code

As mentioned earlier the federal government recently implemented a series of major changes to the Code as well as reinforcing some existing provisions. These changes were made with the express benefit of assisting franchisees and to give confidence to those considering entering the sector. They included the following:

General

- More disclosure information by the franchisor at the start of the franchise including a simpler disclosure statement. Any new franchisee must ensure that he receives this new disclosure statement which is much more transparent than previously.

- A disclosure statement must now provide that like any business, the franchise or the franchisor can fail, and this could have consequences for the franchisee.

- Franchisors will be required to give franchisees six month's notice if they do not intend to renew a franchise agreement. If the term of the franchise is less than 6 months then only one month's notice is required.

- Franchisors will be required to disclose to all prospective franchisees more information on unilateral contract negotiations or confidentiality obligations.

- Franchisors must also disclose whether there are any requirements for the franchisee to pay a franchisor's legal costs incurred in a dispute resolution.

Variations to past and future franchise agreements

- For franchise agreements entered into in the financial year that started on 1 July 2011, 1 July 2012 or 1 July 2013, the franchisor must now disclose the circumstances in which the franchisor unilaterally varied a franchise agreement since 1 July 2010. After 2013 the variations in the past 3 years must be shown.

- Franchisors are now required to disclose the circumstances in which they may unilaterally vary the franchise agreement in the future

End of lease term and franchise agreements

Franchisors are now required to disclose any details of the arrangements that will apply at the end of the lease term including the following:

- Whether the franchisee will have any options to renew the franchise, extend the scope of the franchise agreement or enter into a new agreement. If so what process will the franchisors use to determine this?

- Whether the franchisee will be entitled to an exit payment at the end of the franchise agreement and if so how this will be determined.

- Whether the franchisee will have the right to sell the business at the end of the agreement. If so whether the franchisor will have first right of refusal and how the market value will be determined.

- How capital expenditure during the term of the agreement will be taken into account at the end of the agreement.

If you buy a franchise business from another franchisee which may have been started prior to 1 July 2010 you may not qualify for these new amendments so please check this.

Capital expenditure reforms

Franchisors under the new Code will be prevented from requiring franchisees to undertake significant capital expenditure without notice or justification However a franchisee may require the franchisee to undertake significant capital expenditure, unless one of the following exceptions apply:

- The expenditure is enclosed in the disclosure statement before entering into or renewing or extending the term or scope of the agreement.

- The expenditure is to be incurred by all or a majority of franchisees and such expenditure is approved by the majority.

- The expenditure is as a result of legislative obligations.

- The expenditure is agreed to by the franchisee.

- If such expenditure is in the view of the franchisor to be necessary it must be justified in a written statement given to each affected franchisee. It must show the rationale for the investment, the amount, the anticipated benefits and the expected risks associated with making the investment.

The role of the ACCC in managing the code

- The role of the Australian Competition and Consumer Commission (ACCC) and the powers given to it under the new Code is to strengthen the local industry and to be a watchdog.

- It has already given warning to rogue franchise operators that its new powers gives it the right to seek significant penalties for serious Code breaches.

- As from 1 January 2015. the ACCC has new powers to issue infringement notices and seek penalties up to $51,000 in court for serious breaches of certain Code provisions.

- In addition, the ACCC now has new powers to conduct random audits of franchisors to ensure that they comply with the law.

- Franchisors will now have to update their procedures to ensure that they comply with the new Code and adhere to procedures as set out in the Code.

12

Interference by the landlord in the rights of the retailer

Even if retailers have a lease which gives them the right to quiet enjoyment during the lease term, landlords always has the right to improve the value of their property. This may take the form of a landlord relocating the retailer to another tenancy in the centre, demolishing the retailer's premises or even closing a car park that supplies the retailer with a lot of traffic flow.

The State Acts allow the landlords to do this but each action has consequences and the landlord is expected to compensate the retailer. Let us now look at some of these interferences and how to negotiate them to your best advantage

Relocation during the lease term

- With the continuing upgrading and redevelopment of existing shopping centres, landlords will not hesitate to invoke their right under the lease to move you to a new location in the centre, but remember that no retailer should allow themselves to be pushed around and should be prepared to invoke the protection given to them under the State Acts for such actions.

- Always try to have a relocation compensation clause for the fixtures and fittings that will be abandoned in the old store included in the lease. Some of the Acts now set out the amount of the compensation payable. These new compensation sections in the

Acts therefore become a deterrent to the landlord to "move you at will", solely to satisfy a tenancy mix requirement.

- Try to add a proviso in the lease so that the landlord will be responsible for all moving costs, including the costs of setting up temporary premises whilst your new location is being prepared.

- You should also request that a clause be added that makes provision for the waiving of your responsibility for the de-commissioning of your old store.

A more detailed look at compensation provisions if a landlord disrupts a retail business

NB: Acquainting yourself with this information can mean money in your pocket.

The lessor "is liable to pay" the lessee reasonable compensation for loss or damage suffered by the lessee if the lessor, or a person acting under the lessor's authority acts in any of the following ways:

- He relocates the lessees business to other premises during the term of the lease or any renewal of it.

- He substantially restricts the lessee's access to the leased shop.

- He takes any action (other than action under a lawful requirement) that substantially restricts or alters access by customers to the leased shop or the flow of customers to the retail shop.

- He causes significant disruption to the lessees trading in the leased shop.

- He does not take all reasonable steps to prevent or stop significant disruption within his control.

- He does not rectify as soon as possible any breakdown of plant or equipment under the lessor's care and maintenance, or any defect in the retail shopping centre or leased building containing the leased shop. (The exception is a defect that is due to a condition that would have been apparent to the lessee when he entered into the lease or when he/she accepted of assignment of the lease).

- He neglects to clean, maintain, or repaint the retail shopping centre or leased building containing the leased shop or the part of the centre or building that under the lease is the lessor's responsibility.

- He causes the lessee to vacate the leased shop before the end of the lease or renewal due to the extension, refurbishment or demolition of the retail shopping centre or leased building containing the leased shop.

- **Section 43(2) of the Queensland Act further provides that:**

"The lessor is liable to pay the lessee reasonable compensation for loss or damage suffered by the lessee because the lessee entered into the lease or a renewal of it, on the basis of a false and misleading statement or representation made by the lessor or any person Acting under the lessor's authority or the leased shop was not available to the lessee for trading on the specified date in the disclosure statement because of the default of the lessor or anyone Acting under the lessor's authority"

How the amount of the compensation is decided?

The amount of compensation payable in the previously mentioned situations will be decided by way of the dispute process. Any provision in a lease is void if the landlord tries to limit the amount of compensation payable under this section.

If the retailer believes that any of the above situations have occurred, he should immediately notify the lessor of his intentions to take action under the Act. The amount of damages will be determined later.

Usually the amount to be claimed is "the gross profit that would have been earned on any fall of sales, compared to the same period in the previous year."

13

Leasing pitfalls in upsizing
your existing retail store

Lease implications of upsizing retail premises

In an attempt to compete with large power stores, more and more speciality retailers are upsizing their premises. This often is achieved by either taking over the store next door when the lease on that store expires or by building onto the existing premises.

However, with the increasing number of sales on the internet and the number of retailers implementing their own websites, it may be a time to reduce rather than upsize your premises.

Lease negotiation considerations

Any action to upsize could affect the lease on your existing store. Tenants who embark on this course of action should take the following into account:-

* When breaking down walls between two previously separate premises, always re-measure the total size of the premises. Often the new shop is not the sum of the two store sizes as provided in the individual leases and ends up being a different size.

* Rentals per square metre for larger stores are often lower than for speciality stores. Therefore, if you have upsized to a larger store, it is critical that you negotiate your rental for the combined premises with the landlord. The new agreed rental should recognise the

change in size. Do not simply add the rental paid on the new store to your existing store to arrive at the total rent payable.

- Ensure that the city council is aware of the consolidated status of the new store and you are assessed for rates and taxes accordingly.

- It is critical that the original lease is varied so that rental adjustments and termination of the lease on both stores are synchronised to a common date.

- Usually the upsizing of a store will entail the investment of a substantially increased amount of stock. This may also mean that you need a storeroom facility in the centre to carry reserve stock holdings.

- Try to negotiate acquiring a storeroom by way of a licence agreement to run simultaneously with the new lease and which starts and ends on the same dates.

- Usually storeroom facilities should be on a rental only basis with no outgoings payable on this area.

- Apart from the problems involved with renegotiating your lease, you need to fully assess the financial viability of an upsizing operation.

Financial considerations and costs

- Statistics show that doubling the size of the retail store will not necessarily result in a doubling of your turnover.

- The larger area will also require the retailer to keep a larger stock holding in order to adequately stock the new retail store.

- Unless arrangements can be made with suppliers to finance any additional stock holdings, substantial working capital will have to be provided by the retailer from their own financial resources.

- A larger retail store will more than likely require a complete new refit of the new premises with very little being salvaged from the existing retail store.

- Based on current costs, this could mean a large financial investment by the retailer which is likely to involve borrowing from a bank or financier.

- Fit-out costs will have to be amortised over the life of the lease and the projected profitability of the new" super" retail store will have to be sufficient to absorb any reduction in equity and produce cash flow to repay the lender over the lease term.

- The servicing of a larger area requires an extra point of sale terminal as well as hiring staff to service any additional customers that will be drawn into the enlarged retail store.

- The retailer will not only have the cost of additional staff, but staff will have to be available on Sundays and public holidays with the cost of penalty rates.

- A larger open style "super" retail store where customers select their goods and bring them to the cash registers makes the store more vulnerable to stealing. The retailer may either have to introduce additional security measures or be prepared to sustain a possible increase in stock shrinkage.

- When assessing the potential sales for a "super" retail store, it is important to remember that in a shopping centre, where you may have one or two other similar retailers as competitors, you may not be able to sell more of a particular line than you are currently selling simply because you have a larger area. This may mean that you may have to introduce additional lines and departments.

- Often new lines or departments carry a higher element of risk and unless you can find lines that will yield a higher gross profit than you are currently earning from the total retail store, these new departments can eat into your store profitability.

- Larger retailers have proved to be very successful in some major shopping centres but often they have been established as "mini majors" from day one and not upsized from a smaller retail store.

- Possible deregulation of the pharmacy industry as proposed by the new Competition Review Report may well also act as a break on upsizing of pharmacy type retailing in the future.

However if after consideration of all the facts you still wish to upsize then I hope that at least you will now be cognisant of the possible pitfalls and dangers of this course of action.

14

A lease for retail premises where you own the property (from which you run your business)

Improve the value of your family assets

The value of the property to a landlord is determined by the rent a retailer pays. The rent is then capitalised by a valuer at a percentage that is the yield an investor would be looking to receive from that property.

This yields ranges from 6% for a large shopping centre to 12% for smaller properties depending on their location.

For Example:

In a property that a retailer owns and from which he trades has a capitalisation value of 10%, and he pays himself a notional $50,000 per annum in rent, the value of the property is:

$$\frac{\$50,000}{10\%} \quad \text{(This is how property valuers and property owners would express this equation)}$$

$$= \$500,000$$

Against such a valuation a bank may be willing to advance the retailer 75% by way of a mortgage. He can therefore borrow 75% of $500,000 or $375,000 to acquire another property or invest it in his business.

He then has a valuable asset that he can underpin by entering into a lease between himself and an entity owning the property and thus have the ability to raise extra capital if he wishes.

If the business can afford it he can then raise the rental further increasing the capital value of the business.

This is a good method of using the lease to improve the value of family assets.

15

Initiating an early lease negotiation with a landlord

Retailers are often faced with the dilemma as to when to start to negotiate a new lease with their landlord.

- Often the "gut" feeling is to leave the negotiation as close to the termination date of the lease as possible in the hope that rentals will be lower at that stage. This may not turn out to be a good negotiation technique.

- If you begin discussions about 2 months before the end of the lease you may find that the negotiations become protracted. You may start to panic about running out of lease time and accept terms and conditions in your lease which can later become onerous.

- For example, if you are contemplating the sale of your retail store and you have only two years to go with no further option, it is imperative that you initiate negotiations with your landlord for a new lease as soon as possible.

- The longer you leave it the more difficult it will be to achieve your desired outcome. It is also very difficult to sell a retail store with a lease with only a short term to run on it.

Impact of declines in retail sales on negotiating techniqes with landlords

From my observation, the wave of publicity given to the problems experienced by small retailers on radio, television and in the press, has begun to have a possible effect on leasing negotiations with landlords. These include:

- The demand by landlords for a fixed annual increases of 5% per annum has now in a number of cases been watered down to CPI or to CPI levels plus a fixed percentage of about 1.0%.

- More and larger fit-out contributions are now being offered to retailers, particularly in new centres or in the redevelopment of existing centres.

- Relocation compensation formulas are now becoming standard in leases.

- More and more small retailers are achieving promotional rental rebates thereby reducing rentals for up to twelve months until trading conditions in a shopping centre improve.

- Market reviews are more often than not achieving much lower rentals in centres with known trading problems.

- Requests by retailers to introduce retailer favoured clauses are becoming more easily accepted by landlords.

- But even more important for landlords, the basis used by many valuers to value property has now moved away from applying a cap rate to the current rental but rather to the net present value of future rentals.

- Therefore, a long lease with the type of rentals paid by a retail store has additional importance to the landlord in the valuation of his property for the purposes of future bank borrowings.

- Opening negotiations with a landlord to initiate a new lease should not be a fearful exercise on the part of the retailer but rather an opportunity to reset the level of occupancy cost for a number of years to come.

The right time to negotiate an early lease renewal – for both retailers and landlords

From my experience the best times to open early negotiations include the following:-

For Retailers

- At anytime during the lease term, providing you believe that it will give you an advantage, you will be able to take advantage of any falling rents, restore or extend the term of your lease, gain one further option period or even allow you the opportunity to bring your lease under the new retail tenancy legislation in your state.

- The strategy is to find an opportunity to initiate such an early lease renewal, which will give you an advantage but will also be beneficial to the landlord as well.

- If the lease calls for a market review where there is no "ratchet clause" in the lease that could result in a fall in rental for the landlord.

For Landlords

- On the change of retail tenancy legislation in your state where the new act contains further rights for the landlord that are beneficial.

- If a centre is being redeveloped and the landlord wishes to relocate the retail store.

- On the termination of any exclusivity condition in your lease to allow further similar retailer to trade in the centre.

16

Relief against forfeiture of the lease where a landlord locks out a retailer

This chapter applies in the main to Victorian retailers.

Whilst some states have some form of relief from forfeiture, if the landlord locks a tenant out, the state of Victoria has some special provisions of which the tenant should be aware. They are the following:

- In the event of a lockout from the retail premises, under section 89 of the Act, VCAT is the only body that can hear a claim by a retailer against a landlord for relief from forfeiture.

- Even though the landlord may have grounds for locking out the retailer, the retailer may seek relief from forfeiture via this section, providing he promises to fix the issue that caused the lockout.

- In addition, since section 92 provides that each party must pay its own costs, the landlord may not recover legal costs from the retailer. Thus a landlord may win but actually lose.

This is a very useful defence for a retailer who is being threatened with a lockout by the landlord. Therefore the landlord or his agent should become fully familiar with the implications of this provision of the Act.

17

Negotiating with your landlord during an economic downturn

In the current economic climate, given falling retail sales, what avenues are open to the tenant to try to reduce overall occupancy costs?

Retailers whose rents are up for renewal at the moment are generally in the "box seat". Not many landlords are able to increase rents substantially on renewed leases and some rents are even decreasing.

In the current climate retailers should not be afraid to ask for a rental abatement.

Negotiating techniques

One of the most successful ways of getting a rebate is by writing a well-reasoned letter to the landlord setting out your position arising from the economic downturn and requesting a temporary rental rebate.

An example of a typical letter requesting a rebate from a landlord could be on the following lines:

The Landlord
ABC Shopping Centre

Dear Sir

Re Lease of XYZ Pty Ltd at the ABC Shopping Centre

As you are no doubt aware retail trading conditions in Australia have deteriorated substantially over the past few years with most retailers experiencing lower sales and reduced margins. Our category of retail sales is no exception.

Our performance at the above centre has now reached a level at which we have no choice other than to seek some form of rental abatement from you. This abatement will hopefully assist us in the short term until retail conditions improve at the centre.

We are thus proposing the following for your consideration:

1. That we be provided with a rental abatement of $xxxx per month either by way of a credit on our rental statement or by way of an advertising concession. This abatement to be for a period of six months, when the continuation of the abatement can be reconsidered.

2. We will continue to pay our share of outgoings and marketing levy as per the lease.

3. Any rental increases due prior to the next six months will be waived and forgiven..

Looking forward to a favourable response to our request

Yours Faithfully

Other useful negotiation techniques

For those retailers who are about to renegotiate their leases, the following leasing tips will I hope ensure that you will be able to put into place a lease that will see you through the downturn and that will stand you in good stead over the next five years:

- Do not be afraid to ask for a substantial rental reduction at the start of the new lease. Landlords will be reluctant to lose tenants who pay their rent regularly.

- If your lease is due to expire in the next few months, ask for the first two years of the new lease term to be fixed at the agreed level with the first increase to be at the start of the third year.

- To overcome any landlord objections insert a market review at the end of the third year of the lease, which will allow the rental to be restored to market rent if the economy has recovered by that time.

- Many retailers have a storage area within the retail store that is not used for displaying goods. Do not be afraid to split the area of the retail store in the new lease. For example, split the store into a 10m^2 a store room and a 140m^2 display area. The display area rent will be consistent with current rentals and the storage area will be consistent with current storage rates (e.g. $200 per square metre) with no outgoings payable for this storage area. This will reduce the overall rental cost for the two areas.

- Instead of entering into a new lease, ask for the current lease to be varied for a further two years at the same or reduced rental. As a result you will avoid the necessity of a refurbishment of the store. You will also have a saving in working capital which is difficult to obtain in the current climate.

- Request that the landlord increases his contribution to the promotion fund to attract more traffic flow to the centre.

- Use the opportunity to vary your "permitted use" to include other usages for the retail store.

- Take the opportunity to again request for an option to be inserted in the lease that will assist with the resale of the retail store in the medium term.

- Request the landlord to provide you with a fit-out contribution to any type of fit-out to the store that will be undertaken. This may be merely a cosmetic change to your store but it will enhance it for a possible sale down the track.

18

Types of shopping centres

Leases are not the same and neither are shopping centres. The rent that you may have to pay for a similar store may differ vastly depending on the classification of each shopping centre.

The classification is in turn dependant on the size of the centre, the major tenants, the annual turnover of all tenants and the traffic flow to that centre. If a shopping centre has a department store like Myers or David Jones, it has a higher ranking and commands a higher rental than if it's major tenants consist of only discount department stores like Kmart, Target or Big W.

The number of supermarkets in a centre as its anchor tenants can also determine the rent paid under the lease.

In most publications dealing with shopping centres the following termination is usually used:

Regional Centres: These are major integrated retail centres under a single management with at least one department store or discount department store of a minimum of 10000 square meters. The centre will have a total reporting gross lettable area (GLA) in excess of 25000 square meters. If it has three discount department stores (DDS) with a minimum of 5000 square meters in size and a GLA of 50000 square meters it can be considered as a regional centre.

- **Top 10 Regional Centres:** These are the ten highest ranked regional centres based on total reported turnover.

- **Sub Regional Shopping Centre:** These usually consist of two major DDS and one or more supermarkets.

  Double DDS Centres: A type of sub regional centre with 2 DDS.

  Single DDS Centres: A type of sub regional centre with 1 DDS.

- **Supermarket Based Centres:** These are usually less than 10000 square metres and comprise of one or more major supermarkets along with a collection of food and non-food speciality shops and services in the same enclosed area.

- **Central Business District Centres (CBD Centres):** These are centres located in the central business district of Australian capital cities with either a national major or have a significant arcade in their own right.

19

How to administer leases in a portfolio

The setting up of an occupancy cost control document is essential for the proper administration of a lease portfolio. If a retailer is sufficiently successful and has more than five stores maintaining of a schedule is essential.

There are a number of helpful software packages on the market that offer this information. If you do not wish to go to this cost, you can set up a simple Excel spread sheet on your computer. If kept up to date, this will provide you with all the information that is required to monitor and administer occupancy costs.

The document will be linked to a separate spreadsheet that monitors the moving annual turnover of each store in your network. It sounds complicated but is easy to work with and delivers precise information and is therefore of great value.

What do we mean by moving annual turnover (MAT)?

This is a term often used in retail. It refers to the turnover of the store for the 12 months to the present date. Therefore on 30 April 2015, the moving MAT becomes the 12 months to 30 April 2015. Once we know the May sales, we add this to the moving annual turnover figure and deduct the May sales of the previous year.

How to set up an Excel Spread Sheet

Three vertical line items are allocated to each store

The following information is entered in each column about each store:

Store Location and store number	
Store Size:	xxx square metres
Base Rent:	$ Total Base Rent per lease $ Base Rent per square metre – by dividing total base rent by the store size
Percentage Rent:	Calculated on an ongoing basis as per formula in the lease
Total Rent:	Adding base rent to Percentage Rent
Rates and Taxes:	Rates and taxes on an annual basis. Some landlords charge monthly, others quarterly and, again, others annually.
Outgoings:	Enter total outgoings as per landlords estimate for the store.
Marketing Contribution:	Enter the total contribution as per landlord's estimate for the store.
Total Occupancy Cost:	Total Dollar value calculated by adding total rent, rates and taxes, outgoings, and marketing contribution. By expressing the total occupancy cost as a percentage of the moving annual turnover, we have the occupancy cost to sales percentage for that store. By dividing the total occupancy cost by the store size we now have the total occupancy cost per square metre
Sales MAT:	This is obtained by transferring the MAT from the attached spread sheet to this column for each store
MAT per Square metre:	This is calculated by dividing the MAT by the store size.

Lease Commencement Date:	As per lease
Lease Expiry Date:	As per lease
Lease Term And Options:	As per lease
Date when Option Must Be exercised:	As per lease
Date of last rent review:	As per lease
Details of last rent review:	As per lease. However if increase was waived or reduced by the landlord, this should be recorded here.
Date of next Review:	As per lease
Mode of next Review:	This is either be a sum fixed as per the lease, a percentage increase, CPI or a market review. If the lease ends on the date of the next rent review, enter either "new lease" or "store closure".
Calculation of percentage rent:	This is usually a percentage of sales less base rent or a percentage over and above a threshold figure.
Guarantee if and by whom:	As per lease
Special conditions in lease:	As per lease. Also include notations here like "lease incentive for example, $20000 payable" storeroom rent at $1000 per annum" or outgoings over base year 2014". If we have the information available we could add these 3 additional columns.
Centre traffic Flow:	As per information in Shopping Centre News etc.
Centre MAT:	As per information in Shopping Centre News etc.
Spend Per Visitor to our Store:	Calculated by dividing our store MAT by centre traffic flow

20

Option renewals and exercising an option under the terms of the lease

Not many major landlords are prepared to offer tenants an option in their leases. However smaller landlords who are trying to secure a good tenant for a long period are prepared to offer options in leases.

If you have secured a lease with an option there is a distinct process you need to go through in order to exercise such an option. The process is as follows:

- Your management schedule will alert you to the date by which you have to exercise your option.

- Remember that an option in a lease is a right that the tenant has and not the landlord.

- The tenant alone can decide whether he will exercise the option or not.

- Until you formally exercise the option, the landlord may be uncertain whether you will continue in occupation or whether he will have to find a new tenant, perhaps even at a reduced rental.

- Providing you ensure that you do not miss the deadline date, you could use the opportunity to improve your conditions in the lease by requesting the landlord to vary certain of the conditions in the lease as part of the option exercising process.

- Remember that taking advantage of the landlord's vulnerability at this stage can often result in variations to clauses in the lease that are currently to the tenant's disadvantage.

- The ability of the tenant to take advantage of this situation will be decided by how the original option terms of the lease were negotiated.

- If you are able to negotiate options to renew the lease make sure that they are not restrictive.

- Never accept a clause that grants an option stating that the landlord could cancel this option if he wishes to redevelop or refurbish that part of the centre.

- To be on the safe side, you should always retain the right to exercise your option to take up premises in an alternate site in the centre. This applies particularly if there is to be a redevelopment of the centre involving your store.

- Avoid clauses in leases where the landlord demands "due and punctual performance" of all of the terms and conditions of the lease throughout the term as a pre-condition to the exercise of an option.

- Be sure to have your solicitor water down such a clause as outlined previously to enable you to exercise the option provided you are not in breach of the lease" at the time of the notice" exercising the option or at the expiration of the term of the lease, This does not apply to some minor breach during the term of the lease which you may have already rectified

LETTERS TO LANDLORD EXERCISING THE OPTION

If you do exercise the option for a further term, the retailer *must under no circumstances* write a conditional exercise of the option.

An example of letter you do **not** write

"In terms of clause 4 of the lease, we hereby exercise our option for a further term of 3 years providing we can arrive at a lower rental than at present".

This is a conditional exercise of the option and if the landlord so desires he may argue that you have not exercised your option.

This is an example of letter that you **do** write

"In terms of clause 4 of the lease, we hereby exercise our option for a further term of 3 years.

Then a day or so later you may write the following letter to the landlord.

"As you are aware we have exercised our option for a further term of three years. However, we are unhappy with our present rental and before we proceed to market value as per the lease, we would like to meet with you to discuss a possible lower rental".

21

What constitutes retail premises under the protection of the Retail Leases Act in Victoria?

In all states other than Victoria the premises that fall under the Act are usually listed as a schedule to the Act in that state. However, this is not the case in Victoria.

In Victoria, the section of the Act dealing with retail premises is complicated, due mainly to the wording of the Retail Leases Act. Therefore much interpretation is involved. Each lease has to be assessed individually. As this is a complex area a consulting specialist in the field is often your best course of action.

The Small Business Commissioner in Victoria issued the following guidelines on what constitutes retail premises in Victoria.

The statement verbatim

I have set out the following guidelines in full for the benefit of retailers and other businesses that may offer goods or services for sale, for example legal and accounting firms. The statement must be read in conjunction with section 4 of the Acts. Retailers and other providers of goods and services should read the statement carefully before entering into a lease in Victoria.

The criteria for determining whether the premises are "retail premises" are set out in section 4 of the Act. The premises will be "retail premises" if the premises, or part of the premises, under the terms of the lease, are used are to be used wholly or predominately for the sale or hire of goods by retail or the retail provision of services (section 4(1) (a)).

Further, section 4(1) (b) provides that the Minister may determine that a specified business or specified kind of business is "retail" for the purposes of section 4.

Note, the word "lease" which is used in section 4(1) is defined in section 3 of the Act as meaning a lease, sub lease, agreement for lease or sub lease whether or not in writing.

Guiding principles to determine "retail premises"

The Act does not define "retail". Therefore an interpretation of the term must rely on its ordinary meaning. Therefore in order to determine whether the premises are "retail" each lease must be assessed individually, having regard to the nature and provisions of the lease, including the actual or intended use of the premises under the terms of the lease, and the actual circumstances in this respect.

The following guidelines derived from leading decisions of the Tribunal and courts are provided to assist in assessing whether the premises are "retail" premises". Express or implied prohibition on retail use:

If the lease expressly or impliedly prohibits retail use of the premises, there is an assumption that the premises are not retail. An example of an implied covenant prohibiting retail use of the premises is a covenant requiring the tenant to comply with planning requirements and lawful use of the premises. For example, the local law and/or planning laws may prohibit the premises from being used as retail - that is, the premises may be located in an "industrial" zone.

How the premises are "used, or are to be used"

In the absence of an express or implied prohibition, the way the premises are used, or are to be used, under the terms of the lease must be taken into account.

Actual usage may, in some circumstances, assist in the interpretation of the terms of the lease in this respect, but cannot contradict them. From the language of section 11(2) of the Act, it would appear that the way the premises are used or are to be used is assessed at the time the lease is entered into). For some leases, there may be no actual use at the time the lease is entered into.

For example when an agreement for lease is signed for the purpose of erecting a building on the premises, the commencement date of the lease is the date the works are completed and the premises are ready for trade. In these situations, the use is assessed according to the express or implied terms of the lease (this may be found in the "permitted use" clause).

However if it is unclear from the permitted use clause whether a retail use is permitted, and the landlord and tenant are in dispute as to whether the premises are to be used for retail purposes of a particular kind or kinds, the Tribunal or a court (as the case may be) is likely to explore what the intentions of the landlord and tenant were when they entered into the lease to the extent that this intention can be determined objectively, that is, that the parties cannot give evidence as to their subjective intention.

Sale to the "ultimate consumer"

The provision of goods or services generally involves a sale to an "ultimate consumer". This is the ordinary meaning of "retail" consistent with definitions found in various authoritative dictionaries. These dictionary definitions indicate that it is implicit in the concept of "sale" that goods are sold at a price, which involves the payment of *money. The position is similar with respect to the meaning of "hire" (i.e. "hire" does not mean merely "lend", gratuitously, as "sale" does not involve "giving" in the usual sense).*

The ultimate consumer is generally a member of the public; however the ultimate consumer can also be a class of persons. For example, a retail shop selling books and information products that are only sold to members of a certain professional association would still involve a sale to the "ultimate consumer".

In respect of the kind of sales made to the ultimate consumer, many, if not most are for household or personal use. However the meaning of "retail" is not limited to these situations and may include large commercial transactions, providing they are made to the "ultimate consumer".

It should not be overlooked that the definition of "retail" in the Act also includes the hire of goods and, additionally, includes the retail provision of services and therefore the "ultimate consumer" test is also to be applied to these classes of retail, as indicated by previous Tribunal and court decisions.

These decisions do, however, indicate that the retail provision of services may take place in circumstances where, for example, professional services are provided for an intermediary where the "ultimate consumer" pays for those professional services and the nature and content of the "product" of those services is not changed in any substantial way by the intermediary. An example is the professional advice of a patent attorney which is provided to a firm of solicitors on behalf of their client where the advice of the patent attorney is passed on to the solicitors' client.

Sales in small quantities may be retail

If the premises are used for the sale of goods in small quantities to the "ultimate consumer", this may be indicative of the sale being "retail". However, the quantity of goods sold is not necessarily a decisive factor.

Retail excludes wholesale

The concept of "retail" excludes sales by wholesale. Wholesale sales are the converse to sales to the "ultimate consumer" discussed above, as commonly wholesale sales are to retailers, industrial, institutional and commercial users. These recipients acquire the goods for the purpose of resale to others who will be the ultimate consumer, of a retail sale.

Also, premises where wholesale sales are carried out, such as factories or warehouses, are generally not premises where the public are invited, and are not places where retail sales are expected to be made to the ultimate consumer. Note however that factory outlets, or second's shops, in factories or warehouses are likely to be exceptions as they involve retail sales.

Example:

A hardware shop selling nuts and bolts to the general public would be "retail premises", whereas a warehouse selling nuts and bolts to hardware shops would not.

Similarly, an industrial premise where nuts and bolts are manufactured, and sold to distributors, who then sell their products to wholesalers, would not be "retail".

Occupancy costs"? – The $1 million dollar rule

If the lease exceeds $1million dollars in rental it may be excluded from the provisions of the Act.

The term "occupancy costs" is defined in section 4(3) as being the total of:

- *the rent (excluding turnover rent);*

- *outgoings of a prescribed kind; and*

- *other costs of a prescribed kind*

payable under the lease. Outgoings of a prescribed kind and other costs are set out in regulation 7 of the Regulations (see paragraph 9.4 below).

Lease incentives included as "rent"?

Rent reductions, abatements, or other lease incentives provided for under a separate deed to the lease may not be considered effective to reduce the amount of rent payable under the lease for the purpose of calculating "occupancy costs" as the deed may be considered an anti-avoidance mechanism, and runs the risk of being made void if disputed under sections 94(2) and (3) of the Act.

What are "prescribed" outgoings and costs?

Regulation 7 of the Retail Leases Regulations 2003 prescribes the kind of outgoings and other costs for the purposes of sections 4(3) (b) and (c). The prescribed outgoings are as follows:

- *amenity facilities, including gardening and landscaping, public address and music systems;*

- *building or retail shopping centre management services, including temperature control, insurance, pest control and ventilation;*

- *communication facilities, including telephones and post boxes;*

- *customer facilities, including car parking, lifts, escalators, and child minding;*

- *hygiene services, including cleaning, garbage collection and disposal, sewerage and waste disposal;*

- *information services, including customer traffic flow and other building intelligence information, information directories and signage;*

- *rates, taxes, levies, premiums, charges and fees, including municipal council rates and charges, sewerage and drainage rates and charges, administration costs, audit fees and management fees;*

- *repairs and maintenance services;*

- *security services, including emergency systems and fire protection equipment; and*

- *utility services, including electricity, gas, oil, water and energy management systems;*

The prescribed other costs are as follows:

Advertising and promotional services, including marketing fund contributions. These outgoings and costs have been prescribed for the purpose only to calculate the "occupancy costs". Therefore, outgoings which fall outside of these categories will not be included in the calculation of "occupancy costs"; however they can be recovered from the tenant, provided they do not otherwise offend the Act.

This means that there may be leases that have a total liability for costs in excess of $1,000,000 per annum which still come within the application of the Act. That is, the total liability for costs is made up of a component of prescribed occupancy costs which is less than $1,000,000, and a component of other non-prescribed costs which, *in addition to the total of prescribed occupancy costs, exceeds $1,000,000.*

Time occupancy cost is calculated.

It appears from section 11(2) of the Act that the total occupancy cost is to be calculated at the time the lease is entered into. However, when leases are entered into, some of the actual costs are unknown. Actual costs may become known only at a later point during the first term of the lease. The question this raises is whether the total occupancy cost should be calculated on the actual costs, or the estimated costs.

In cases where the occupancy cost borders on the $1,000,000 threshold, it would be unreasonable for the parties to wait until all actual costs are ascertained before it is known whether the lease is subject to the Act or not. This would also create a burdensome administrative task of refunding or back-charging the fees that are prohibited from being recovered under the Act.

In the circumstances, it appears that practical necessity dictates that an estimate of costs at the commencement will be sufficient. Of course, the estimated costs should be reasonable, and where ascertainable, have regard to last year's actual costs.

The commercial premises exception

Leases of commercial premises take many forms, for example, professional suites, head administration offices, and call centres. Some commercial premises will fall into the definition of "retail" by virtue of the way the premises are used, as opposed to the lease's permitted use, which is often termed "office".

On the other hand, some leases will involve a use of the premises merely for office purposes where no retailing is involved. These may include leases of premises to management or administration companies that provide a service to a retailer or other intermediary (as opposed to the ultimate consumer). Therefore for example, the "head office" premises to a fashion retailer or the office of the master franchisor may not be retail.

However this may differ where the office is an essential component of the retail business, particularly where customer orders or enquiries are handled from that office. In this instance, the office may be considered "retail".

The Minister's Determination

A lease of premises where the retail provision of services occurs would, in the first instance, be a "retail premises" to the extent that the criteria in section 4(1) (a) are satisfied. However, the Minister has made a Determination limiting the application of the Act to these "commercial leases".

The Determination made for the purposes of section 4(2) (f) and published in the Victorian Government Gazette No. s 75 (30 April 2003) provides as follows:

Premises not constituting retail premises

This determination is made under Section 5(1) (c) of the Retail Leases Act 2003. This determination does not apply to:

- *premises that under the terms of the lease relating to the premises or part are used, or are to be used, wholly or predominantly for the sale or hire of goods by retail; o*

- *retail premises located in a retail shopping centre.*

Acting under Section 5 (1) (c) of the Retail Leases Act 2003, I determine that the following kind of premises are premises to which Section 4(2) (f) applies:

Premises that are located entirely within a building which, under the terms of the lease relating to the premises, or part of the premises, are used, or are to be used, wholly or predominantly for the retail provision of services, other than premises located entirely on any one or more of the first three storeys in a building, excluding any basement levels.

This determination comes into effect on 1 May 2003.

This Determination excludes premises or part of the premises in a building that are used wholly or predominately for the retail provision of services, other than those located on any one of the first three storeys of the building. In calculating the first three storeys of the building, the basement levels are not included.

The Determination does not affect the application of the Act to any premises in the building which are used wholly or predominately for the retail sale of goods. The Determination also does not affect any premises in a retail shopping centre which are used wholly or predominately for the retail provision of services (and for the retail provision of goods for that matter). These types of premises are still "retail premises" within the meaning of the Act, providing that the criteria in section 4(1) are otherwise.

Practical tips for calculating stories

The third storey of the building may not necessarily be the third floor of the building. That is, if there is a "ground floor", this would be counted as the first storey. Similarly, what is called the "basement" level in the building's directory or elevator may not be a basement in the ordinary sense of the word. "Basement" is ordinarily taken to mean the car park level or the storage level, which is usually uninhabitable. But in some office buildings, the "basement level" is occupied by tenants, commonly by food court tenants, travel and real estate agents, beauty salons, newsagencies, etc. So how are the storeys to be calculated? intended that the use of the term "excluding any basement levels" is for the purpose only of calculating the three stories. It is irrelevant that there may be retail premises located on a "basement" level. Retail premises located on the basement levels will still come within the Act. Therefore to assist in determining the first storey (which then allows the calculation of the remaining 2 stories) the first floor above the storey which is categorised as "basement" should be established. In most cases, this will be the "ground" floor, or if there is no ground floor, the "first" floor. A simple way to determine this is to have regard to the way the stories are described in the building's tenant directory or elevator.

Some examples:

- *The directory describes a medical suite as being located on "Floor 3". The floors of the building are "Basement", "Floor 1", "Floor 2", and "Floor 3". In this example, the relevant three stories of the building, excluding the basement levels, are ""Floor 1", "Floor 2", and "Floor 3". As the medical suite is located within the first three stories of the building, the Act will apply to the medical suite premises and any other retail premises in the building.*

- *The directory describes a hairdresser as being located on the "Basement". The floors of the building are "Basement", "Floor 1", "Floor 2", and "Floor 3". In this example, the hairdresser is located on a basement level. Accordingly, it is not necessary to determine the relevant three stories of the building. The Act will apply to the hairdresser's premises and any other retail premises in the building.*

- *The directory describes an accountant's practice as being located on "Floor 2". The floors of the building are "Basement 2", "Basement 1", "Ground 1", "Ground 2", "Floor 1", and "Floor 2". In this example, the relevant three stories of the building, excluding the basement levels, are "Ground 1", "Ground 2", and "Floor 1". As the accountant's practice is located above the first three stories of the building, the Act will not apply to the accountant's premises*

- *The directory describes the car park (which involves a paying service) as being located on "Basement 1 – 3". The floors of the building are "Basement 3", "Basement 2", "Basement 1", "Ground", "Floor 1", and "Floor 2". In this example, the car park is located on the basement levels. Accordingly, it is not necessary to determine the relevant three stories of the building. The Act will apply to the car park premises and any other retail premises in the building.*

- *The directory describes an architect's firm as being located on the "Mezzanine". The floors of the building are "Basement", "Ground", "Mezzanine" and "Floor 1". In this example, the relevant three storeys of the building, excluding the basement levels, are "Ground", "Mezzanine" and "Floor 1". As the architect's firm is located within the first three storeys of the building, the Act will apply to the architect's premises.*

- *The directory describes a law practice as being located on "Floors 2 and 3". The floors of the building are "Basement", "Ground", "Floor 1", "Floor 2", "Floor 3" and "Floors 4-10". In this example, the relevant three storeys of the building, excluding the basement, are "Ground", "Floor 1" and "Floor 2". As the law practice is not located entirely on one or more of the first three storeys of the building, the Act will not apply to the law practice.*

It is clear that each building must be considered in isolation, and a common sense approach employed in each instance.

Definition of "retail premises" – changes from the   previous Acts

Franchises

Provided that the contractual arrangement that the franchisee holds with the franchisor is a lease or sublease, and all the criteria in section 4(1) are satisfied (see paragraph 6, above) and none of the exemptions in section 4(2) apply (see paragraph 8, above), the premises will be *"retail premises". This is in contrast to the 1986 Act and the 1998 Act which excluded franchisees from the application of those Acts if the tenant operated under a name or mark identifying, commonly associated with or controlled by the landlord.*

Carrying on a business

It is not a requirement for the application of the Retail Leases Act 2003 that the tenant is carrying on a "business" of retailing in order for the premises to be considered "retail" pursuant to section 4(1) of the Act. The only requirement under the Act in this respect is that the tenant is permitted to use the premises for retailing "under the terms of the lease" (see section 4(1)). This is in contrast to the 1986 Act and the 1998 Act which required the tenant to be "carrying on of a business involving" retailing. Therefore tenants who operate not-for-profit organisations (for example, op-shops) are now clearly included in the application of the Act.

Part of premises

The definition of "retail premises" in the Act now contains the additional words "or a part of premises" which seemingly widens the scope of premises included in the application of the Act.

Although it is not free from doubt, it would appear that the effect of the addition of these words was intended to be limited to accommodating mixed retail and residential use of premises as contemplated by section 95 of the Act (which makes provision for maintenance in good repair of the residential area where the Residential Tenancies Act 1997 does not apply). An interpretation of these provisions which applied the "wholly or predominantly" test in section 4(1) with respect to part only of the premises would produce a far broader application of the Act – beyond what would generally be regarded as retail premises – than Parliament would be likely to have intended. For example, this interpretation of the Act would capture leases where the premises are used almost exclusively for wholesale, industrial, manufacturing or office uses but which also contain a small retail outlet occupying a very small part of the premises where sales to the public are undertaken.

In borderline cases, it may be unclear whether the premises are used wholly or predominately for wholesale, manufacturing, industrial (etc.) purposes or whether the premises are used wholly or predominately for the retail sale of goods. Consider for example, a dairy manufacturing premise that contains a manufacturing part and a retail sales part, both of equal area. In this case, it is unclear what the premises are used wholly or predominately for. It would therefore be advisable to at least treat the retail part as a "retail premises". This can be done by drawing up two leases, one for the "retail premises" and the other for the manufacturing area. In the alternative, one "retail premises" lease can be drawn up that covers the whole of the premises - this will be easier to administer than having two leases for the premises.

When "retail premises" determined

As discussed above, section 11(2) of the Retail Leases Act 2003, in effect, provides that the time for determining whether the premises are "retail" is at the time the lease is entered into or renewed (see sections 7 and 9 for definition of "entered into" and "renewed" respectively). This is in contrast to the 1986 Act and the 1998 Act which did not contain such a provision. Under these Acts, the applicability of the Act could be affected throughout the term of the lease and therefore could cease to apply or begin to apply at any time during the lease term.

Because of the effect of section 11(2), if the Act applies to the lease when entered into or renewed, and subsequently there is a change in circumstances during the term of the lease that affects the applicability of the Act, the lease will remain subject to the Act. Similarly, where the Act does not apply when the lease is entered into, the lease will not become subject to the Act if there is a change in circumstances affecting its applicability. Therefore the status of the applicability of the Act is determined at the outset and does not change during the term of the lease. Examples of the circumstances that may change include an increase (or decrease) in the total occupancy cost, or the tenant becoming (or ceasing to be) a listed company.

As such, the only opportunity for the status of the applicability of the Act to change is upon renewal of the lease. For example, a lease is entered into with a public company tenant for five years with a five year option for renewal. At the time the lease was entered into, the Act did not apply. In year 3, the lease is assigned to a non-public company. There is no variation to the terms of the lease and therefore the assignment does not amount to a new lease (section 8 of the Act). For the remaining two years of the initial term, the Act will not apply. However, upon the lease renewal (because the renewal of a lease is regarded as the granting of a new lease), the applicability of the Act changes and the Act may then apply to the lease for the five year option term. The same would apply if the lease term were extended by agreement. This results in a surrender and termination of the existing lease and the grant of a new lease for the remainder of the then extended term.

Thus it is essential when entering into a lease for a tenancy in a CBD building selling goods and services and you want the protection of the Retail Tenancy Act that you pick one of the first 3 floors of that building.

22

Who is responsible for paying for the legal costs in preparing a lease and the stamp duty on a lease?

The law relating to who is responsible for paying the legal costs of preparing a lease and the stamp duty on a lease payable to the State Government, varies from state to state. This could be a substantial cost to a new retailer as he may have to pay his own legal costs as well as the legal costs of the landlord. These costs need to be taken into account in your decision to enter into the lease.

New South Wales

A tenant is not liable to pay for lease preparation costs except any amendments to the lease that are requested or negotiated.

It is worth noting that a tenant cannot be compelled to use a lawyer nominated by the landlord.

No stamp duty is payable on leases.

Victoria

The landlord cannot charge the tenant for legal costs and other expenses relating to the negotiation, preparation and execution of the lease nor for the costs of obtaining the mortgagees consent nor the landlord's requirement to comply with the Act.

This does not preclude the landlord recovering the legal costs in respect of an assignment of the lease, including the investigation of the proposed assignee.

No stamp duty is payable on leases.

Queensland

The landlord cannot charge the tenant the legal costs for preparing, renewing or extending a lease.

The landlord can however charge the tenant for the registration of the lease, survey fees associated with the registration of the lease, obtaining the mortgagees consent, the costs of any actual variation to an ongoing lease and the landlord's consent to a sublease or licence.

No stamp duty is payable on leases.

Australian Capital Territory

Each party must bear its own legal costs. However, if the tenant wishes to have the lease registered under the Land Titles Act he must pay for registration costs of the lease and the costs of obtaining the mortgagee's consent.

It is worth noting that a tenant cannot be compelled to use the lawyer nominated by the landlord.

No stamp duty is payable in the ACT.

I would recommend that all leases be registered if you are opening a store in the ACT.

Northern Territory

A tenant is liable for only reasonable legal expenses incurred by the landlord. He must however be provided with an account showing how the amount has been calculated. This must also be shown in the disclosure statement.

A landlord can recover legal costs from the tenant where the prospective tenant enters into negotiations and then withdraws.

It is also worth noting that a tenant cannot be compelled to use the lawyer nominated by the landlord.

Stamp duty is not payable.

South Australia

The tenant is required to pay one half of the landlord's legal costs unless he withdraws from the negotiations. If the retailer withdraws he may be required to pay the full amount.

The tenant is expected to pay mortgagees consent fees.

The tenant is not required to pay anything unless he receives a detailed account of how the charges are made up.

No stamp duty is payable.

West Australia

The act is silent on this issue and therefore will have to be negotiated between the parties. I would recommend that each party pays its own legal fees.

No stamp duty is payable.

Tasmania

A tenant is not liable to pay for lease preparation costs except where any amendments to the lease that are requested or negotiated.

A landlord can still recover legal costs from the tenant where the prospective tenant enters into negotiations and then withdraws.

Mortgagees fees are payable.

It is also worth noting that a tenant cannot be compelled to use the lawyer nominated by the landlord.

No stamp duty is payable.

23

Conclusion - checklist of tenants rights under the Retail Leases Acts

As indicated in earlier chapters the Retail Tenancy Acts in the various states and territories give the tenant rights and protection from landlords. They also stop landlords from requesting certain clauses in leases which are unreasonable. The acts also aim to create a level playing field during the negotiation process.

Whilst this chapter is not meant to be a legal lesson and you will need to consult a lawyer in most cases, it is crucial for tenants to have this information available when negotiating a lease with a landlord. Though some points may have been included earlier, they are worth repeating. The checklist is again broken up by state as the law is different in each state. We will be looking at the three major states of Victoria, New South Wales and Queensland.

Victoria

- There is no specific list of premises attached to the Victorian Act as indicated previously. However you are considered to be a retailer and fall under the act, if you use the premises predominantly for the sale or hire of retail goods or services, the lease is for more than one year, you are not a subsidiary of a public company listed on a world stock exchange and the total occupancy cost does not exceed $1m.

- The landlord is responsible for the repair of the premises, provided that any damage has not been caused by negligence of the tenant. The landlord may not recover the cost of any repair though the outgoings schedule.

- The landlord has an obligation to make statistical information about the performance of a centre available to the tenant.

- A copy of the proposed lease and a copy of the information brochure must be given to the tenant before any negotiations commence. A disclosure statement and a copy of the final lease are required at least 7 days before the lease is entered into. If you do not receive a disclosure statement, the tenant after giving notice to the landlord may withhold rent.

- If the premises are not available for handover on the date specified in the disclosure statement, the tenant is not liable to pay rent.

- The landlord must give a copy of the signed lease back to the tenant within 28 days after receiving a copy of the lease from the tenant.

- If the lease is to be for less than 5 years the tenant must request the Small Business Commissioner to certify a shorter term.

- A tenant in a shopping centre is not responsible to pay for outgoings relating to capital costs, depreciation, sinking funds for capital works, interest on landlord's borrowings, rent under a head lease, rent for other properties and land tax.

- The tenant is not expected to provide his turnover figures unless the lease contains a percentage rent clause.

- Goods and Services Tax must be deducted from sales provided by a landlord to a tenant in respect of percentage rent sales.

- A provision in a lease is void if it prevents the rent falling in the case of a market review of rent.

- A tenant is not required to pay "key money" for entering into a lease.

- If the lease contains an option, the landlord must notify the tenant the date after which the option is no longer exercisable, at least 6 months and not more than 12 months before that date. If the landlord does not give the notice required, the option remains exercisable until 6 months after the landlord gives the required notice. The lease will then continue under the "holding over provisions" of the lease.

- A clause in a lease is void if it prevents the tenant from joining a tenants association.

- The Shop Trading Reform Act makes lease provisions void if they require the trade on Sundays. Remember undue influence or pressure from the landlord, to trade on Sundays may amount to unconscionable conduct.

- Any party to a lease can initiate a dispute. All retail tenancy disputes are initially handled by the Small Business Commissioner's office by way of mediation. Costs of mediation are shared in proportions agreed to by the parties, or if they cannot agree, equally. If mediation as certified by the Commissioner has failed, then it may be referred to the Victorian Civil and Administration Tribunal (VCAT).

- Tenants cannot be held liable to indemnify landlords beyond the liability they would have had in Common Law.

- If the tenant is required to pay a security bond, it must be held in a separate account and the landlord must notify the tenant about all interest earned. The bond forms part of the overall security for the tenancy, which is refundable at the end of the lease.

- The landlord cannot reasonably refuse a bank guarantee in place of a security deposit.

- A provision in a lease requiring the tenant to undertake any promotion or advertising of the tenant's business is regarded as void. However, the tenant may still be required to pay an amount into a marketing fund together with other tenants in order to promote the centre. The tenant is entitled to receive from the landlord a marketing plan one month before the start of each accounting year. In the case of an opening promotion contribution, details of the proposed expenditure must be made available to the tenant, one month before the promotion.

- Neither a landlord nor a tenant can engage in unconscionable conduct. The Act sets out a list of examples of what is considered unconscionable conduct. However, under the Act, it is not considered unconscionable conduct, if the landlord institutes a dispute, fails to enter into a lease or renew a lease or does not agree to have an independent valuation of a current market review. Remember that a tenant has 6 years to issue a claim with VCAT for loss or damage sustained by a landlord for unconscionable conduct.

- If the leased premises or the building in which they are located are damaged, the tenant does not have to pay rent or outgoings. If repairs to the building are impracticable, the tenant or the landlord may terminate the lease.

- If the landlord has to carry out works in the building that affects the tenants business, 60 days' notice in writing to the tenant is required. If the premises have to be demolished the Act in section 56 sets out a detailed formula as to how the tenant is to be compensated,

- If the tenant is to be relocated to a new tenancy, again the Act sets out the conditions under which such relocation is to take place.

- A lease cannot be terminated simply because the tenant has not achieved a certain level of sales.

- The Act has a ban on a restriction on trade if a tenant also trades in premises outside the centre.

- A lease provision is void if it limits the tenant's rights to engage persons doing work on the premises other than under the specified limits of competence and complying with any award affecting the shopping centre.

- A provision in a lease is void if it requires the premises to be refurbished unless it indicates the nature, extent and timing of the refurbishment or refitting.

- If the lease contains a right for the tenant to use part of the premises as a residential area and the Residential Tenancies Act does not apply to the lease, the landlord must ensure that the residential area is maintained in good repair.

New South Wales

- If the store is over 1000m² in size, it does not fall under the Act. However, public companies under this size do fall under the Act.

- Leases for under 6 months in duration do not fall under the Act. The use of the technique of retaining a tenant whilst the centre is under construction must be watched by a retailer. It gives the tenant no protection for compensation during this construction phase. If you have to take out this type of lease, insist that it be for 6 months and 1 day.

- Premises that form part of the office tower of a shopping centre do not fall under the Act.

- There is no obligation to pay rent and for the tenant to take possession of the premises, unless the landlord has completed the fit-out.

- Unlike the situation in Victoria, the creation of a sinking fund for future repairs and maintenance is permitted in New South Wales.

- Land Tax is permitted to be charged to tenants in this state. However this is based on a single ownership basis which is more favourable to a tenant. At the time of writing there have been moves to stop land tax being charged to tenants under the Act in that state.

- If there is a market review in a lease, this must be completed 3 to 6 months prior to the date any option is to be exercised.

- In the case of promotion and advertising charges for a centre, the landlord must provide a marketing plan, a list of expenditure and an account for any unspent contributions.

- A copy of the lease and a retail tenancy guide must be provided to the tenant when negotiations commence otherwise a fine is imposed on the landlord. If the tenant does not receive a disclosure statement at least 7 days before the lease is entered into a fine is imposed. The same applies to a renewal.

- The tenant is not liable for fit-out costs, services, equipment, refurbishment or refitting if these are not disclosed in the disclosure statement.

- A lease can be terminated by the tenant within 6 months of the lease being entered into, if the landlord fails to provide a disclosure statement, or if the statement is incomplete, or materially false or misleading.

- A copy of the lease is to be given to the tenant within I month of registration of the lease subject to the time it takes to obtain the mortgagees or head lessor's consent.

- The tenant has no liability to pay for any fit-out costs or equipment, refurbishment or refitting if they are not disclosed in the disclosure statement. The tenant is not liable to pay for fit-out works that are more than the agreed maximum amount.

- A provision in a lease, requiring the tenant to undertake any promotion or advertising of the tenants business are regarded as void. However the tenant may still be required to pay an amount into a marketing fund together with other tenants to promote the centre.

- The landlord must provide the tenant with a statement every 6 months concerning expenditure from any promotion or advertising fund. If this is not provided the tenant can withhold any contributions to the fund until it is received. Any unspent money must be carried forward to future expenditure.

- A lease cannot be terminated simply because the tenant has not achieved a certain level of sales.

- The Act also has a ban on a restriction on trade if a tenant also trades in premises outside the centre.

- Rental increases of CPI plus a percentage are allowed in New South Wales but not in Victoria.

- A provision in a lease which prevents the rent falling on a market review is regarded as void.

- If the parties cannot agree on the market rent, then the Act allows the retailer to apply to the tribunal to set the market rent.

- If the tenant must be relocated in a shopping centre, he is entitled to payment by the landlord of the reasonable costs of relocation.

- A landlord can withhold his consent for the assignment of the lease if the assignee proposes to change the usage or the assignee, has financial and retail skills inferior to the assignor or has not complied with the lease.

- Key money cannot be requested for consent.

- Goods and Services Tax must be deducted from sales provided by landlord to the tenant in respect of percentage rent sales.

- A guarantor is no longer liable on the lease, if the person assigning the lease for an ongoing business, has handed over a copy of the disclosure statement to the assignee.

- A clause in a lease is regarded as void if it prevents the tenant from joining a tenants association.

- If the tenant is required to pay a security bond, it must be lodged with the Rental Bond Board within 20 days after receipt of the bond. Both the landlord and tenant must sign any application to pay out money from this account.

- The landlord cannot reasonably refuse a bank guarantee in place of a security deposit.

- If the leased premises or the building in which the retailer is located is damaged, the tenant does not have to pay rent or outgoings. If repairs are impracticable to the building, the tenant or the landlord may then terminate the lease.

- If the landlord has to carry out works in the building that affects the tenant's business, 90 days' notice in writing to the tenant is required. Section 34 sets out the formula for compensation to be paid. If the premises have to be demolished the Act in section 35 sets out a detailed formula as to how the tenant is to be compensated. It is wise to familiarise yourself with these provisions.

- A lease provision is void if it limits the tenant's rights to engage persons to do work on the premises other than specifying limits of competence and complying with any award affecting the shopping centre.

- A refurbishment requirement is void unless it sets out in general terms, the nature, extent and timing of the refurbishment.

- Where the tenancy is part of a strata subdivision, the Act extends some of the provisions applicable to body corporates and centre managers. Some of the bylaws of a body corporate may also apply to the lease. Tenants are advised always to ask for a copy of the body corporate bylaws to ascertain if there are any liabilities that may be passed on to the tenant, particularly major repair, and maintenance and body corporate fees.

Queensland

- If the store is over 1000m^2 in size and is leased to a public company it does not fall under the Act.

- Stores over 10,000m^2 in size leased to any person or company also do not fall under the Act.

- The Act also does not apply to franchised service stations governed by the Petroleum Retail Marketing Franchise Act.

- Leases for fewer than 6 months are exempted from most of the provisions of the Act.

- A lease can be terminated by the tenant within 6 months of the lease been entered into, if the landlord fails to provide a disclosure statement, or such statement is incomplete, or materially false or misleading

- Within 30 days after signing the lease the landlord must supply the tenant with a certified copy of the lease. If the landlord fails to do this he can be fined.

- Unlike the other states where 5 years is the minimum lease period that must be offered to the tenant, Queensland has no minimum period for the lease.

- In the event of a specialist valuer being used to determine the market rent for the premises, each party must pay for half the valuer's fee.

- Land Tax is not recoverable from tenants if they fall under the Act.

- A landlord can charge a tenant for the supply of electricity to the premises based on charges under the Electricity Act in that state. Tenants should always request that the rate for electricity should be at the same rate as paid by the landlord or the best rate.

- Where the tenant supplies the landlord with sales figures for percentage rent purposes, the landlord may not disclose these figures other than those as provided in the Act.

- Unlike Victoria that allows for only one form of rental increase, Queensland permits rental increases to be CPI plus a percentage. A cap on the CPI is permitted under the Act. For example CPI shall be not more than 4% or less than 2%.

- If the lease has a market review of rent clauses and if the parties cannot arrive at a figure, the review must be undertaken by a specialist valuer in a manner as set out in the Act.

- If a retailer is buying a business from an existing retailer and the lease has an option for a further term and the lease provides for a market rent review on the exercise of such option, the tenant in order to facilitate the sale, may request an early determination of a review in writing. Any notices in this regard must be not more than 6 months or less than 3 months from the date on which the option is to be exercised.

- Whilst sinking funds are permitted for major repairs and maintenance, any annual sinking fund payment must not exceed 5% of the total estimated outgoings and the balance in the sinking fund may not at any time exceed $100,000.

- Payment of key money to secure a tenancy is prohibited.

- Rent in advance is limited to one month's rent.

- If a tenant suffers damage as a result of actions by the landlord that disrupt trade or limit access to the premises, the Act sets out how compensation is to be paid even if the tenants is in a: "holding over" period after the expiry of the lease term.

- A landlord may not impose additional restrictions on an assignment of the lease.

- An existing tenant and the guarantor are automatically released from the lease if on assignment a disclosure statement is provided to the assignee and on condition that any such statements are not misleading or defective.

- If the lease contains an option, the landlord must notify the tenant as to the date after which the option is no longer exercisable at least 6 months and not more than 12 months before that date.

- If the landlord does not give the notice required, the option remains exercisable until 6 months after the landlord provides the required notice. The lease will then continue under the" holding over" provisions of the lease.

- A clause in a lease is void if it prevents the tenant from joining a tenants association.

- A provision in a lease that attempts to force a tenant to trade outside the core trading hours is void. In addition, tenants who do not open their stores are not liable to pay the extra outgoings caused by the tenants that do remain open.

- Disputes about the lease are settled firstly through mediation, and if the dispute is not settled after 4 months, it is referred to the tribunal where each party pays its own legal costs.

- Unlike in Victoria, the lease can provide that a tenant may have to indemnify a landlord for any damage suffered by the landlord as a result of the tenant's actions.

- Unless a retailer has more than 6 stores in Australia he may be requested to provide a financial advice and legal advice report to the landlord. A consultant will be of assistance in completing these reports.

The Retail Tenancy Acts in the above 3 states are currently under review by the state governments. Any prospective retailer should consult an attorney to ascertain whether the tips suggested in this book are still valid or whether case law and the Act has changed.